HEROES OF TENNESSEE

Volume 1
The Tennessee Series

HEROES OF TENNESSEE

edited by
Billy M. Jones

MEMPHIS

Memphis State University Press
Memphis, Tennessee

TABLE OF CONTENTS

CONTRIBUTORS

ROBERT E. CORLEW, the Dean of the School of Liberal Arts at Middle Tennessee State University, is among the foremost authorities on the state's history and is widely recognized for his many excellent books and articles on the subject.

ILENE J. CORNWELL, author of *Footsteps Along the Harpeth,* currently is Director of Publications for Vanderbilt University Medical Center. She served for 4½ years as Information Officer for the Tennessee Historical Commission.

CHARLES W. CRAWFORD, Associate Professor of History at Memphis State University and Director of the Oral History Research Office, is a leading authority on Tennessee history and the author of numerous books and articles.

WILLIAM J. CROCKER, Director of Foundation Studies at Northwest Junior College in Senatobia, Mississippi, and a resident of Memphis, is an authority in the areas of folklore and poetry.

EMMETT ESSIN, who received his Ph.D. in history from Texas Christian University, currently is Professor of History at East Texas State University.

BILLY M. JONES, President of Memphis State University, is the author of numerous books and articles in history.

WILLIAM R. MAJORS, Professor of History at Motlow State Community College in Tullahoma, Tennessee, currently has a manuscript in Press at Memphis State University on Gordon Browning.

JAMES L. MOODY, JR. is Director of the Historic Pensacola Preservation Board: ROBERT M. McBRIDE is Editor of the *Tennessee Historical Quarterly.* Both are prominent in the study and writing of Tennessee history.

J. RALPH RANDOLPH, Associate Dean of the College of Arts and Sciences at Memphis State University, is the author of two books in history and formerly was an Associate Professor of History at Southwest Texas State University.

ROBERT V. REMINI, the foremost authority on Andrew Jackson and the recipient of numerous grants and awards, currently is Professor of History and Research, as well as Professor of Humanities, at the University of Illinois, Chicago Circle.

RONALD N. SATZ, currently Dean of Graduate Studies and Research at the Unviersity of Tennessee at Martin, also is an Associate Professor in the Department of History. Among his many publications are *Tennessee's Indian Peoples* and *American Indian Policy in the Jacksonian Era.*

INTRODUCTION
by Billy M. Jones

*T*ennessee is a land rich in geography, containing mountains and valleys, lakes and rolling hills, towering pines and entangling shrubs. Its climate varies from alpine cool to sweltering heat, which allows the Volunteer State to be known for its ski facilities as well as its summer resorts. Tennessee is equally rich in its heritage, which stretches from Indians whose past is shrouded, to Spanish and French explorers, to a present rich in promise. Finally, Tennessee is rich in human resources, for it has been singularly blessed with resident and native sons and daughters who have pioneered not only in this state but also who pushed on westward to settle much of the rest of the American frontier. Many of these Tennesseans lived lives of quiet heroism—working, hoping, dreaming, looking at their children and wanting something better for them. However, some performed deeds of such outstanding merit that they earned from their descendants the designation "hero."

A hero, says Webster in the *Third New International Dictionary* (1971), is "a man of courage and nobility famed for his military accomplishments, an illustrious warrior." However, Webster wisely understood that all heroes are not military figures or great fighting men, and he added to his definition that a hero also can be "a man admired for his achievements and noble qualities and considered a model or ideal," as well as "the central figure in an event, action, or period."

The great lexicographer was correct in giving several definitions for the word hero. Some of those included in this volume are remembered as military figures and illustrious warriors: Andrew Jackson, Nathan Bedford Forrest, and Alvin York, men who won

enduring fame in battle; others, however, are affectionately re-
called and revered for giving up their lives voluntarily: Sam Davis,
who chose hanging rather than betraying a friend, and Casey
Jones, who stayed with his train and died in order that others might
live; yet others achieved the status of heroes by saving lives without
having to sacrifice their own: Nancy Ward, who warned settlers of
impending raids, and Tom Lee, who could not swim but pulled 32
victims of a steamboat disaster from the mighty waters of the
Mississippi; and, finally, some are remembered and deemed heroic
by the scope of their deeds: Daniel Boone, Davy Crockett, John
Sevier, and Sequoyah.

Tennessee's heritage is so rich that the process of selection for
this volume was difficult. Other sons and daughters of the state
might easily have been included, men and women whose deeds, in
the words of Webster, were "noble" and worthy of being "considered a model" by those who have inherited the great traditions of
the Volunteer State. In looking back at these individuals, we find
members of both sexes and all races, people who fulfilled their destiny, who kept faith with their neighbors, their dreams, and their
God. It was they who transformed Tennessee from a frontier wilderness into a vital part of the United State and helped mold the
character of a nation.

We of today should not conclude that the age of heroism is
past, that people now can find nothing against which to test themselves. For those who look closely, there still are problems to challenge, still questions that demand answers. There are mountains to
cross, rivers to ford, and hardships to overcome—although a different nature from those encountered by Tennessee's first pioneers
and overcome by its heroes. If we imitate the deeds and accomplishments of those whose biographies are included here, we
likewise can transform our state—and nation—this time from a
wilderness of the spirit to a place where words such as "equality"
and "opportunity" and "freedom" have full meaning. Should we
accomplish these tasks, we can win for ourselves the epitaph "hero"
and be worthy of imitation by our descendants.

1

DANIEL BOONE
by Emmett Essin

Daniel Boone, one of the greatest hunters, explorers, and pioneers of the 18th century and a legend to all subsequent generations of Americans, was not an exclusive hero of Tennessee. But then he likewise was not an exclusive hero of North Carolina, Kentucky, or Missouri. Rather he was a hero of all these states—and of the nation. As a precursor of civilization, Boone served as one of the great men in advancing the American frontier. He and men like him made it possible for Americans to wrest a significant portion of the Old Southwest from the Indians and Spaniards.

In popular literature, and recently through the mass-media, Boone has been portrayed as a primitive man who gave up civilization for the solitude of forests and mountains, a man who was more at home alone in the wilderness or with the Indians than with his fellow men. He also has been described as an effective leader of pioneers; he blazed trails for others to follow, chose strategic sites for homes and forts, and guided numerous families to the dark and bloody grounds of Kentucky and later across the Mississippi River to Missouri. He was a brilliant Indian-fighter, a man who knew the ways of the Indians and, more important, could match their skill in warfare. As do most stereotypes, the above contains much that is true, for it accentuates the attributes of Boone in a special way. But Boone the man was more complex than he appears in the stereotypes. Neither myths nor historians have explained why Daniel Boone was forever restless, forever moving from place to place with reckless abandon.

Daniel Boone, the sixth son of Squire and Sarah Morgan

Boone, was born on October 22, 1734, in Oley Township, Pennsylvania (Berks County, a few miles from Reading). At the time of his birth, the Boone family had lived only 17 years in the Colony of Pennsylvania. Daniel's grandfather George, a weaver from Exeter, England, had immigrated with his family to Philadelphia in 1717. From there the family had moved to Quaker communities in Pennsylvania.

Much of Daniel's early childhood is shrouded in myth, but when he was 10 years old family records reveal that Squire purchased 25 acres of grazing land several miles from the Boone home, and that Daniel accompanied his mother and the Boone's cattle to the newly acquired acreage. There mother and son spent the entire grazing season—from early spring to autumn—living in a small cabin while Squire remained at home managing his blacksmith shop and small weaving establishment. Daniel was to spend the next six summers in this pastoral setting.

Late in life Boone was asked how he had learned to exist alone in the wilderness, and he attributed much of his knowledge of the ways of the forest and his prowess with weapons to those leisurely spent grazing seasons. Each morning he drove the family herd into the fields, and each evening he herded them back toward the cabin to be milked. All day he wandered and hunted in the surrounding forest. At age 12 his father gave him a short-barreled rifle. Within a year he was the main provider of wild meat for the family. By age 15 he was, according to his own recollection, the best shot in Berks County.

In 1750, Squire and his family left Oley Township for the Colony of North Carolina. On May 1, the Boones set out westward across Pennsylvania, through Carlisle, and down the Cumberland and Shenandoah Valleys. When they reached Winchester, they decided to pause for awhile. Squire set up his blacksmith shop and found accommodations for his family. Daniel and his friend, Henry Miller, were soon exploring and hunting game all the way to the headwaters of the Yadkin River. After a year of hunting and trapping, they sold their furs in Philadelphia for $1300, spent several weeks in the city, and returned broke.

The next year the Boones were on their way again, arriving in the Yadkin Valley early in 1752. Like many who had preceeded him

Daniel Boone. *Photograph courtesy the State Library and Archives.*

to the frontier, Squire illegally squatted on the land he eventually purchased. Not until December of 1753 did he buy land from the Earl of Granville's agent. By that time Daniel had already traveled throughout the wild Yadkin country and had developed a reputation as an extraordinary marksman. Game was everywhere, and a skillful hunter could make an excellent living. Boone trapped otter and beaver and killed buck deer. One buck skin was as good as a dollar and could be exchanged for that amount of goods. On the Yadkin Valley frontier and in later frontier areas as well, the common term for a dollar was a buck.

Shortly after the French and Indian Wars began, 29-year-old Daniel Boone joined the North Carolina militia as a wagoner and blacksmith. Late in 1754 the militia moved to Fort Cumberland on the Maryland border. The next year it was assigned to the ill-fated, ill-planned Braddock expedition to capture Fort Duquesne. It was during this expedition that Boone met John Finley (or Findlay), a trader serving as a wagoner for the Pennsylvania militia. Two or three years before, Finley, traveling down the Ohio River, had been captured by a Shawnee hunting party and was taken to their temporary camp in the Kentucky lowlands. He heard of the warriors' path across the mountains and realized that it passed through the Cumberland Gap. The Gap could be reached from the place where he was being detained. Finley eventually returned to Pennsylvania just in time to join the war effort. Boone listened intently to this trader's descriptions of Kentucky, but possibly he heard equally vivid accounts from one of the scouts of the expedition, Christopher Gist, who had traveled in Kentucky three years before Finley's capture. Or Boone could have learned more from Dr. Thomas Walker, the commissary general to the Virginia militia. Walker had discovered the Gap in 1750 while scouting for the Loyal Land Company of Virginia. Probably, however, wagoner Boone never met Walker.

On the afternoon of July 9, Braddock's expedition was ambushed by the French and Indians. Although almost three times as large as the French and Indians' force, Braddock's army was caught in unfavorable terrain. As Boone later observed, the army had no eyes or ears on the day of the battle. Engineers, not scouts, led the troops across the Monongahela River; the guards on the flanks had been pulled into the main columns; and most of the colonial companies, whose men alone had any experience fighting Indians, were in the rear. Boone, who had just gotten his wagon across the river, was thoroughly disgusted at what he saw. He was ordered to remain with his wagon at all costs, but when he realized the hopelessness of the situation and saw the Indians coming nearer, he followed the lead of the other wagoners, jumped on the lead horse, cut his team's harness straps, and headed the frightened animal back across the river.

The ambush had a profound effect on Boone. Two-thirds of the British-colonial militia force, more than 1000 men, were dead. Later when leading others, Boone always made certain of the terrain and maintained a healthy respect for the Indians. During the Revolutionary War, he would avoid another massacre at the Salt Licks in Kentucky.

After escaping, Boone headed back to the Yadkin Valley, arriving there before the end of August. Within a year, on August 14, 1756, Daniel had successfully courted and married the 16-year-old daughter of Joseph Bryan, Rebecca. The couple lived with the Bryans until Daniel built a cabin and cleared land near a fork of Sugartree Creek. Within two years the Boones became parents of two children (James, 1757; Israel, 1759), and Daniel changed his lifestyle at least for awhile. No longer a hunter and adventurer, he became a scratch farmer; only occasionally was he able to hunt or trap. With his newly added responsibilities, he never stayed away from his young wife and family for long. Occasionally he did attend the militia muster at Salisbury. There he won the shooting matches and almost always lost his prize money on cock fights.

Boone did not envision himself as a scratch farmer for the rest of his life. He wanted to emulate the affluent men he had observed in Salisbury and elsewhere. He was anxious to improve his position—to be a large landowner, a man of wealth and influence. He rationalized that with no formal education, the best and quickest way to realize his ambitions was to become a land speculator—to search out virgin lands west of the mountains, stake out claims, and later sell acreage to incoming settlers. His dreams, he knew, were fraught with difficulties. To realize them, he needed the backing of wealthy men, for he required money to make money.

His chance came in the spring of 1758 when Boone joined the British-American force to capture Fort Duquesne. Again he was to serve as a wagoner. Led by General John Forbes, the army blazed a new trace across Pennsylvania only to discover that the French had abandoned their fortifications.

After this venture, Daniel hurried back to Sugartree Creek, no doubt believing that he was leaving the fighting behind him. That was not the case, however, for in 1759, the Cherokees, with provocation, began attacking white settlements. For several months the Boones "forted up" in Fort Dobbs on the south fork of the Yadkin, but Rebecca, who again was pregnant, convinced Daniel to leave the area until the Cherokee War was over. By that time many Yadkin Valley families had already left. Daniel and his family along with his younger brother, Ned, and his sister and her husband traveled to Culpepper County, Virginia, some 35 miles from Fredericksburg. There for a time he worked as a wagoner hauling crops to market. In November, 1760, Rebecca was delivered of a daughter, Susannah, and within two weeks, Daniel had left to explore, hunt, and trap, leaving Ned in charge.

On this expedition Daniel wandered farther than ever before and crossed the Blue Ridge Mountains. He explored much of East Tennessee, roaming the valleys of the Holston and Watauga. Along a tributary of the Watauga (now called Boone's Creek in Washington County) he paused to carve a message on a beech tree— "D. Boone Cilled A. Bar on tree in the year 1760." Just how much of East Tennessee he explored on this trip is unknown, but he did establish a camp near a deserted cabin (probably somewhere on the banks of the Watauga), and for a brief time he was accompanied by an elderly slave named Burrell.

Returning to Culpepper after checking on his homestead at Sugartree Creek, Boone heard that Virginia and North and South Carolina were forming a large force to defeat the Cherokees and end the war. After he sold his furs and provided for Rebecca and the children, he joined one of Colonel Hugh Waddel's North Carolina militia companies. During this nine-month campaign, Daniel learned first-hand how to break Indian resistance: burn crops and villages, strike suddenly without warning, and show no mercy.

At the conclusion of the Cherokee War, Boone, Nathaniel Gist, and James Norman trapped and hunted all winter throughout southwestern Virginia, eastern Tennessee, and western North Carolina. Gist's father, Christopher, had explored extensively in Kentucky, and during the trip the subject of the Dark and Bloody Grounds surely was discussed. The next spring Daniel returned to the Yadkin to plant a crop. After harvesting it, he finally went to Culpepper County for Rebecca and the children. He had not seen Rebecca for more than a year.

On returning to Virginia, Daniel discovered that all was not well in his family. There was new baby girl (Jemima) in Rebecca's cabin, and when he asked to whom it belonged, Rebecca admitted it was hers and that Daniel's brother Ned was the father. He would never discuss Jemima's birth with Rebecca again and accepted the child as his own. No doubt relations were strained between the couple for some time, but Daniel packed up his family and returned to the Yadkin. Boone and Rebecca would not have another child for four years. After this interlude, Boone left his family more frequently and for longer periods. During the next two years he probably was more at home in the forest than on the Yadkin.

His wanderings, however, were not because of family troubles alone. Daniel, who "had the honor of having more suits entered against him for debt than any other man of his day, chiefly small debts of five pounds and under," had been defended in court by Judge Richard Henderson. Both men liked one another, and Henderson became mildly interested in Boone's plan for obtaining new western lands. To collect his lawyer's fees, he hired Daniel as a land scout.

In August, 1765, Daniel, his younger brother Squire, and his brother-in-law John Stuart (Stewart) joined five of Boone's militia friends for a trip to East Florida. Under the terms of the Proclamation of 1763, the British government had forbidden settlement west of the Appalachian range and had placed the fur trade under strict supervision. To compensate the speculators and pioneers, the British had established the Crown colonies of Quebec, East Florida, and West Florida; and the governor of East Florida had advertised a hundred acres of land free to any Protestant settler. After a harrowing journey, the group reached Pensacola and staked out land claims, although none of them found Florida attractive. It was a strange topography for men of the mountains, and game was not abundant. Boone willingly gave up on the idea of moving when Rebecca vetoed it as being totally out of the question.

After the Florida escapade, Boone's thoughts again turned to Kentucky. With Squire and William Hill, he crossed the mountains into Tennessee, traveled through the Holston and Clinch river valleys, and then followed a branch of the Big Sandy River. The trio speculated correctly that eventually this branch would lead them to the Ohio River. But they turned northward too soon and found themselves on the rugged Cumberland Plateau. They continued their search for the Kentucky lands described by others until a winter snow storm halted their progress. Stumbling upon a salt lick, they made winter camp nearby. Their location was ideal; hunting was unnecessary, for game came to the lick in abundance, especially herds of buffalo. At the first signs of spring, Boone and his companions decided that they had had enough and returned to the Yadkin. They did not know it, but they had been only two day's travel from the bluegrass region they sought.

During the fall of 1768, Boone was planning another assault to find the bluegrass region. By now his debts were mounting, and he had been summoned to appear in the Salisbury court the following March as a defendant in a number of delinquent debt cases. No doubt he thought of the possibility of postponing judgment against him by being able to interest Judge Henderson in his adventure. While Boone was mulling over his possibilities, John Finley arrived in the Yadkin Valley. Now a wandering merchant, Finley was peddling needles, thread, pins, cloth, and other things needed by the women of the frontier. Without much urging the trader agreed to spend the winter with the Boones, and together the two men planned an elaborate expedition. Finley knew he could find the gap through the mountains that had been discovered by Dr. Walker years earlier.

Finley accompanied Boone to Salisbury where both men interested Henderson in the expedition. Again Judge Henderson acted as Daniel's lawyer, had the debt case continued (one account claims that Henderson actually paid off the debts), and advanced the needed capital for the expedition. On May 1, 1769, Boone, Finley,

Stuart, and three hired "camp keepers" (Joseph Holden, James Mooney, and William Cooley) left for Kentucky. Each man rode a horse and led a pack horse loaded with supplies. Henderson had supplied them well. Squire would join them with additional supplies after he harvested the fall crops.

During the initial stages of the journey, they passed through familiar territory. Once in the valleys formed by the headwaters of the Tennessee River, the six men had little difficulty finding Powell Valley—or the Cumberland Gap. Following the well-traveled Warriors' Path, they came to a fork of the Kentucky River (Station Camp Creek). Only a short distance from the path, they established camp, split up into pairs, and began to hunt and explore. Daniel spent the next two years in Kentucky and would not be pleased with all aspects of his adventure. In December he and Finley were captured by a band of Shawnees, but both managed to escape by diving into a canebreak. The Shawnees also found the main camp, which was poorly placed too near the Warrior's Path, and took all the supplies. Soon Finley and the "camp keepers" left for civilization. Late in the autumn Squire and a companion joined the two remaining men. Trouble continued, however, for the adventurers. Stuart failed to return to camp after a hunting trip. (Daniel would find his skeleton two years later in a hollow tree.) The Squire's companion departed for home. That spring Squire left to obtain additional supplies, and Daniel spent the next four months alone exploring. When his brother returned in late July, 1770, Daniel knew more about Kentucky than any other white man. He had wandered as far as the Ohio, along the Kentucky (Louisa), and throughout the Bluegrass region. Not until March of 1771 did the two brothers start home. By then they had their horses loaded with valuable furs. Near Cumberland Gap, they were captured by another hunting party of Shawnees who took their furs, horses, weapons, and supplies. Boone would return to the Yadkin with nothing to show for his two years in Kentucky.

When Daniel returned, he urged Henderson to form a land company and exploit Kentucky. Henderson, although excited by Boone's glowing report, hesitated to commit his funds and those of his friends to a colonizing venture without some sanction from the British Government. Boone's idea was that legalities could wait;

like most Westerners he reasoned that possession was nine-tenths of the law, but Henderson was not convinced.

The next year Daniel moved his family to the Watauga Valley of Tennessee (in or near Sapling Grove), but he returned to Kentucky at least twice. In 1773 he grew tired of Henderson's delaying tactics, gathered together five other Yadkin families and his own, and set out to colonize Kentucky. Along the way Boone's group was joined by another body of Clinch Valley pioneers under the command of Captain William Russell.

The expedition failed, for at dawn on October 10 a small portion of the combined group was surprised by a Shawnee war party. At the time they were within a day's journey of the Gap. Almost all were killed including James Boone, the eldest son of Daniel and Rebecca. After the attack, Boone alone wanted to continue to Kentucky. He had sold all he owned in North Carolina, and, more important, he realized that others less hesitant than his friends were already entering Kentucky and appropriating the best lands. The others, however, would have no more of the venture and returned home. Daniel, temporarily defeated, settled his family for the time at "Snoddy's on the Clinch."

At the beginning of Lord Dunmore's War with the Shawnees, Colonel William Preston, chief surveyor of Fincastle County and a militia commander, ordered Captain Russell to send two "faithful woodsmen" to Kentucky to warn surveyors and others of their eminent plight. Russell chose Boone and Michael Stoner. Both men did as they were asked; within 61 days, they traveled 800 miles. Boone even took time to lay claim to a lot in James Harrod's new settlement before returning. Later that year he commanded three Clinch forts.

With the conclusion of the war, frontiersmen faced one less obstacle to occupying Kentucky, for the Shawnees agreed to give up all claim to lands south of the Ohio River. By now Judge Henderson was ready to act. Others were illegally claiming lands, for even the Shawnee treaty was technically illegal according to British law. Henderson therefore purchased Kentucky land from the last Indian nation that still claimed it—the Cherokee. Henderson's grandiose scheme was to establish a new proprietary colony. With this in mind, he formed the Transylvania Company, and in December of 1774 the would-be proprietor and his backers purchased £10,000 worth of goods and proceeded to Sycamore Shoals on the southern bank of the Watauga River. By March of 1775, more than 1,000 Cherokees had assembled for negotiations. The transfer was concluded on March 17; for £2,000 cash and £8,000 worth of goods, the Cherokees sold Kentucky. By that time Henderson had sent Boone and 30 axemen to cut a road to the new Transylvania Colony. On March 1, Boone began work on the Wilderness Road, starting at Long Island of the Holston River.

When Henderson and the main party of settlers arrived at the location chosen by Boone, the axemen began Fort Boonesborough. They also had taken time to lay claim to the best surrounding acreage. Proprietor Henderson was pleased neither with the fort, which was too small, nor with the "greedy" actions of Boone and the others. But he realized that he could do nothing about the land claims. He also quickly discovered that he was unable to control the actions of his own settlers or those of other men who were establishing stations nearby. Within a few months Henderson left for Philadelphia to secure recognition from the Continental Congress for Transylvania Colony. His efforts were futile; the leaders of Virginia and North Carolina fought the scheme from the beginning and, more important, members of the Congress were discussing the question of independence and were in no mood to recognize a proprietary colony.

A year later Virginia took charge of Kentucky County. Henderson and associates were given 200,000 acres for their efforts and expenses in settling Kentucky. Boone, however, never received the 2,000 acres due him for building the Wilderness Road.

During the turmoil between Henderson and the settlers, Boone had refrained from taking sides. He had never crossed his benefactor. Yet as Henderson's role diminished at Boonesborough, Daniel became the natural leader. As in any frontier community, performance determined reputation, and Boone, a man who knew the ways of the wilderness, was accepted by his fellow settlers.

During the years of the American Revolution, Daniel performed admirably. The Kentucky settlements were besieged both by Indians and British, and for months at a time the people were "forted up." By 1777, unable to raise vegetables, they were existing on nothing but meat and mush, and the meat required salt. On January 8, 1778, Boone led 30 men to the Lower Blue Licks (40 miles from the Licking River) to manufacture salt. The next month, as Boone was returning to the licks with a load of buffalo meat strapped to his mount, he was captured by four Shawnee braves. Taken to their large encampment nearby, he discovered that the Indians were on their way to attack Boonesborough. Boone knew that the fort could never withstand such an assault, for one side of it was not yet enclosed with palisades and the people, not expecting an attack in the dead of winter, would be taken completely by surprise. He therefore made a deal with Shawnee Chief Blackfish. He would surrender his men at Blue Licks as prisoners if they would be treated well and would not have to run the gauntlet. Then he suggested that in the spring the Indians could bring the women and children at Boonesborough to the Shawnee towns to be adopted into the tribe or turned over to the British commander at Detroit, who was offering 20 pounds for each prisoner. Blackfish accepted the offer, and the next day Boone convinced his comrades to surrender.

Boone spent the next five months with the Indians and British. He and the other captives were taken to the Indian town of Little Chillicothe on the Little Miami River. There Daniel and 16 others were adopted by the tribe; the rest were turned over to the British in Detroit. Daniel, now the son of Blackfish, was known as *Sheltowee* (Big Turtle). He accompanied Blackfish to Detroit, impressed the British there, and deceived them concerning the strength of the Kentucky settlements. Daniel enjoyed his life with the Indians, but he also knew that he must escape soon. The British-Canadians were prodding the neighboring Indian tribes into capturing all the settlements in Kentucky, especially Boonesborough; he must warn the people. His chance came on June 16; he made his escape on horseback, rode the animal until it dropped from exhaustion, and then proceeded on foot. He was in Boonesborough in four days after covering a distance of 160 miles.

The rest of the year was a trying time for Daniel. Under his leadership, the fort held out against more than 400 Indians and British-Canadians. Although in actual proportions the victory was a minor one, it was major in the West, for had Boonesborough fallen the other stations in Kentucky would have likewise capitulated, and much of the West would have been in British hands. During the crisis an envious settler charged Boone with duplicity and treason. Tried by a military court, Boone was acquitted and soon was promoted to the rank of major in the Virginia militia. Only after the trial did he go to North Carolina to persuade Rebecca to return to Kentucky. She had left in May, not knowing if her husband was still alive.

Boone would spend almost a year urging Rebecca to go back to Boonesborough. Evidently all was not well with the Boones. Rebecca had heard rumors from Daniel's enemies that during his captivity he had lived with a squaw. In October of 1779 Daniel returned to Kentucky with Rebecca and a new party of Yadkin settlers, including his brother Ned. During his absence Boonesborough had grown, and most of his friends had left or were dead. Shortly thereafter he moved his family to land he claimed five miles from the town. There he built a log house surrounded by a stockade, and it quickly became known as Boone's Station.

In 1780 Daniel's financial affairs, which were never stable, turned far worse. That spring he sold 3,000 acres in order to buy land warrants, giving him the opportunity to survey and purchase larger claims. Before he left to buy the warrants, others who knew him gave him their money for warrants. On the way to Richmond he was robbed of all the money entrusted to him, estimated at between $20,000 and $50,000. Some blamed Boone and asked him to repay them, which he did over a period of several years.

Boone not only brooded over the loss of the money, but also over his brother Ned's death in the fall. Ned, who had married Rebecca's sister, had again developed a close relationship with Daniel since coming to Kentucky the year before. To cap off the year Daniel was appointed lieutenant-colonel of Fayette County and in April of 1781 was elected to the Virginia legislature. Daniel stayed in Virginia for most of 1781, coming home in August for a brief visit and to see his new son Nathan.

During the summer of 1782 Boone served in another Indian campaign. That year the Indians launched numerous attacks throughout Kentucky, so many in fact that Kentuckians referred to 1782 as the "Year of Blood." In a rash retaliation for an Indian raid,

182 men pursued the Shawnee to the Blue Licks. Boone was one of three commanders in charge of the hastily formed expedition. The Indians caught the Kentuckians in a crossfire, killing and wounding many; one of the dead was Daniel's son, Israel.

Israel's death was a severe blow for Daniel and Rebecca, but so too were the beginnings of his land troubles. In 1783 the family was forced to leave Boone's Station. His title was questioned by a newcomer who possessed a certified claim, and the original deed to Boone's Station had been lost when Daniel's agent had been ambushed and killed by Indians. The Boones were forced to move to Marble Creek where Daniel tried farming for a couple of years. At the time Daniel did not consider the loss of Boone's Station as particularly serious. He still claimed thousands of acres—and on paper was a wealthy man.

About the time the Boones left their home, Daniel was interviewed by John Filson, a Pennsylvania school teacher. The next year Filson published an autobiography of Boone in his *The Discovery, Settlement, and Present State of Kentucke.* Written in the worst of late 18th-century style, it became enormously popular and established the Boone myth. Only 33 of the book's 118 pages dealt with Boone's life. Although Boone knew better, he, as an old man in Missouri, would exclaim that the book was "All true! Every word True! Not a lie in it!"

Boone's legend was spread further by Gilbert Imlay. The same year Filson interviewed Boone, Imlay, a smooth-talking land speculator, swindled Daniel out of 10,000 acres of choice land. Giving Daniel a note for £1,000, he later wrote Boone that he had already sold the land and could not redeem the note. Imlay later went to England in order to escape other judgments against him. In 1793 he included Filson's autobiography of Boone in his *Topographical Description of the Western Territory of North America.*

Boone, never content with farming, left Marble Creek in 1786 to become a surveyor and tavernkeeper at Limestone, Kentucky's leading port on the Ohio River, where he remained for three years. It was to be a difficult period in his life. By now others were chipping away at his land claims. For Daniel, Kentucky settlers were becoming as dangerous as Indians. Once he had been the most revered man in Kentucky, but now he was one of the most despised.

Knowing more about Kentucky real estate than anyone else, he frequently was subpoenaed to testify in land suits in which he had no personal interest. In every case, his testimony made another enemy, and at times he was accused of perjury or of being a "chimney corner" surveyor (one who sat in a chimney corner and drew boundaries from memory instead of actually surveying the land). And during these three years he lost thousands of the acres he claimed. He never won a land suit, however, and each time he lost he was forced to sell additional acreage for damages due—sometimes land to which he had but scant claim.

Finally Daniel had had enough. He turned over his business interests to a nephew, John Grant, advised his heirs never to contest any land claims that might be left in his estate, and took Rebecca and Nathan to Kanawha County. There he had a brief respite, for he was among friends. He became a militia commander and in 1791 was elected to the Virginia legislature. During the years he lived in Kanawha County, Boone never really settled down, but hunted and wandered once again in Tennessee and North Carolina. He even took Rebecca and Nathan on one journey back to Pennsylvania.

In 1795, the Boones moved to Bushy Fork near Blue Licks. There Daniel built a cabin on land owned by his son, Daniel Morgan Boone. By now he was a forgotten man in Kentucky; affairs in the new 15th state had seemingly passed him by. In 1798 he felt little pride when the legislature named a county for him. Perhaps the reason was that Daniel had lost his last remaining lands when the sheriffs of Mason and Clark Counties sold the land—more than 10,000 acres—for back taxes.

1798 was the last full year that Daniel Boone lived in Kentucky. The next September the Boones, including Daniel Morgan, Squire, and Jemima and her husband, left for the Spanish territory west of the Mississippi River. They did not have to travel alone, however. Other old friends and relatives who had lost out in the land scramble followed Daniel once again.

The Spanish were expecting the Anglo-pioneers. Four years before, Daniel Morgan had traveled to St. Louis and had spoken with the lieutenant-governor, who had heard of Daniel Boone. That official promised Daniel Morgan, his family, and followers land and for such a distinguished person as Daniel Boone, perhaps a public office, and he had repeated his offer to Daniel in an official letter.

By the end of October, the Boone settlers had arrived in St. Louis. There Spanish officials were waiting to acclaim the Americans, especially Daniel. It was the first time in his life that Daniel had been publicly honored. Now 65 years old, Boone was appointed Syndic (chief administrator including judge, sheriff, and commandant) for a large area west of the Missouri River known as Femme Osage district, given over 800 acres of land (1,000 arpents), and ordered to distribute 400 arpents to each Anglo-American family.

All went well for the Boones during the initial years in Missouri. Daniel still had time to hunt and roam and perform his official duties. He quickly developed a reputation for fairness as a judge. In one case a man and widow appeared before him with a dispute over the ownership of a stray cow. The man had the better claim, but the poor widow needed the cow. Reluctantly, judge Boone ruled in the man's favor. In the next case, however, the judge ordered a disorderly disturber of the peace to turn over one of his cows to the widow as punishment. The brand of justice appealed both to Spanish officials and settlers.

Following the Louisiana Purchase, the Americans were not as generous to Daniel as had been the Spanish. The land commissioners stripped him of all his 1,000 arpents because he had not lived on it or improved it. His explanation that he lived with either of his son's families and that their property joined his did him no good. Boone's children were stripped of 900 acres, approximately one-third of the land they claimed. In 1814, the United States Congress granted to Boone the same amount of land he had had taken away, but that must have been a slight consolation for the 81-year-old man, for all of it had to be sold to meet claims of Kentucky creditors.

Life continued in a normal way for Boone wherever he lived. He still went on spring and fall hunts, but now not alone. He was always accompanied by one of his sons, his son-in-law, or a black servant. In 1812 he volunteered for the second war with Britain, but was turned down because of his age. The next year Rebecca died. In 1815 he visited Fort Osage and trapped for fur in the Yellowstone country. Two years later he returned to Kentucky and paid his last remaining debts. Daniel died at his son Nathan's home on September 16, 1820, just one month shy of his 86th birthday.

During his years in Missouri, Boone was well aware that other men were reworking the events of his life to suit themselves and the public at large. He was becoming more and more a mythical, legendary figure than a real man. The real Daniel Boone deserved but few of the accolades attributed to him by admiring writers interested in selling books. He missed being the first man in the West by more than two centuries, and he was not the first explorer of Kentucky; nor was he a happy wanderer content with the solitude of the forest. However, Boone was an able woodsman and hunter, a skilled diplomat with Indians, a superb Indian fighter when necessary, and a thorough pioneer who possessed more than his share of daring and courage. He never obtained the position in life he had envisioned for himself—a wealthy man of property—but he left a large region settled and prosperous thanks to his pioneering efforts.

SUGGESTED READINGS

The printed material on the life of Daniel Boone is voluminous. In 1901 William Harvey Miner attempted to catalogue the books and articles concerning Boone's life in *Daniel Boone: Contribution toward a Bibliography of Writings Concerning Daniel Boone;* he listed more than 150 books and articles published before 1901. Not until 1902 did Reuben Gold Thwaite write a creditable biography. Entitled simply *Daniel Boone,* it was based primarily on some of the manuscripts of Lyman C. Draper, who spent more than 50 years collecting primary sources concerning the Boone family. This collection is housed in the Wisconsin Historical Society, Madison. The best biography of Daniel Boone is John Bakeless' *Daniel Boone, Master of the Wilderness* (1939). Bakeless' research is impeccable, but he omitted several facts concerning Boone's personal life he thought insignificant. The most recent biography, one that is highly readable, is Laurence Elliot's *The Long Hunter, A New Life of Daniel Boone* (1976). Elliot makes his subject come alive in a special way.

Other historical works concerning Daniel Boone and his surroundings deserving of mention are: Archibald Henderson, *The Conquest of the Old Southwest* (1920); William Stewart Lester, *The Transylvania Colony* (1935); and George W. Ranck, *Boonesborough* (1901). There are a number of short essays or chapters in other works that deal with Boone, his myth and legend. Among the most readable and provocative are "Daniel Boone: Empire Builder or Philosopher of Primitivism?" in Henry Nash Smith, *Virgin Land: The American West as Symbol and Myth* (1950); and "Winning of the Frontier: Boone, Crockett, and Johnny Appleseed" in Dixon Wecter *The Hero in America, A Chronical of Hero-Worship* (1941).

2

JOHN SEVIER
by Robert E. Corlew

John Sevier was probably Tennessee's first "hero," and to say that his career was marked by civil and military accomplishment is to repeat a cliche which nevertheless is well founded. Married and on his own at the age of 16, he was in the vanguard of frontier life and accomplishment until he died in 1815. Governor of the State of Franklin, a six-term governor of the State of Tennessee, and a four-term congressman, he also was a soldier of no mean accomplishment having "fought thirty-five battles [and] won thirty-five victories."

Born near the present town of New Market, Virginia, Sevier, the oldest of seven children, was the son of Joanna Goade and Valentine Sevier. Religious persecution had driven the Xavier family from France to England where the name was Anglicized to Sevier. By 1740, two brothers, Valentine and William Sevier, had come to America, and Valentine had settled in the Shenandoah Valley on Smith's Creek. Soon he was married, and John Sevier was born on September 23, 1745.

Little is known of John Sevier's early years, but he apparently learned to read and write and acquired a fair education for someone living on the frontier where opportunities were limited. In 1761 he married and settled in the vicinity of his birth. There he farmed, dealt in furs, speculated in land, ran a tavern, and fought Indians—along with rearing an ever-increasing family. He apparently moved his place of residence several times; by 1773 he had removed to the Keywood settlement on the Holston River, and three years later to the Watauga, near the present town of Elizabethtown. He became a commissioner of the Watauga Association, and, in 1776 when North Carolina created the "Washington District" from he transmontane settlements, he was chosen as one of three delegates to the Provincial Congress of North Carolina which met at Halifax in November of 1776. He was commissioned a lieutenant colonel in the state militia and was assigned the immediate task of protecting frontier settlements against the attacks of maruding Indians.

The Revolutionary War, of course, had commenced in the preceding year, and Sevier spent much of the next seven years in military activity against the Cherokees and British. The encounter for which he became best known was that of King's Mountain, fought near the close of the War in October 1780, just south of the North Carolina-South Carolina border a few miles north of Spartanburg. After having met with moderate success in the northeast, the British late in 1778 turned to Georgia, the soft underbelly of the colonies, and overran the province without difficulty. From there they moved northward and established bases in South Carolina. Major Patrick Ferguson was assigned the task of protecting the British left flank exposed to the west, and, in the summer and early fall of 1780, Ferguson scoured the Piedmont, destroying cabins of American frontiersmen in his path and winning Tories to his cause. Overconfident, he soon ordered all people living on the frontier to lay down their arms and give allegiance to the Crown; otherwise, he would march his "men over the mountains, hang . . . leaders, and lay the country waste with fire and sword."

Sevier and other frontier leaders, accepting the challenge, gathered troops at Sycamore Shoals late in September and marched westward in search of Ferguson. They soon found him at King's Mountain, a narrow ridge located in the northwestern corner of South Carolina where he, with perhaps 1000 men, had ensconced himself, claiming that even "the Almighty" could not drive him from the height. The American troops ascended the mountain and assaulted the foe from all sides, taking care to remain well camouflaged behind trees, logs, and rocks. Although forced to fall back three times, the Westerners rallied each time and, after about 60 minutes of fighting, claimed victory. They had lost fewer than 100 men among the dead and wounded; they had slain or wounded three times that number, in addition to capturing

Image of John Sevier from *Biographical Album of Tennessee Governors,* copyrighted by J. S. Jones of Knoxville, Tennessee. *Courtesy Mississippi Valley Collection, Memphis State University.*

the remaining 700 as prisoners. Although the victory resulted as much from strategic blunders by the British as from superior strategy on the part of the Americans, it did turn the enemy from the West and enabled Sevier to emerge as the foremost figure among the transmontane people. As Carl Driver, Sevier's principal biographer, wrote in 1932, "It is impossible to state just how great an influence this event exerted upon the career of Sevier."

Hardly had the Revolution ended when Sevier became involved in an independence movement on the Western frontier, which resulted in his being named governor of the short-lived State of Franklin. The North Carolina constitution, drafted in 1776, had provided for eventual statehood for the settlements across the mountains, and the Continental Congress assembling in 1780 had resolved that the western lands of North Carolina and Virginia should become states "at such times and in such manner as Congress shall hereafter direct." As early as 1782, Western leaders had listened to plans by Virginians for transmontane development, and with intense interest had received Thomas Jefferson's presentation to congress whereby the trans-Appalachian country be divided into 18 new states. When in June of 1789 North Carolina ceded to the central government its Holston-Watauga settlements, Western leaders assembled to consider a plan of action. Meeting in Jonesborough in August of 1784, they decided to form a state immediately and thus to be ready for admission to the Union. They chose Sevier as chairman, and, not long thereafter, drafted a constitution and convened a general assembly.

In the meantime, North Carolina authorities had rescinded the cession law before congress could legally accept the land—an act which brought about considerable unrest among Western people. To placate them, the North Carolina legislature pledged additional protection against Indian marauders, created district courts in the frontier counties, and appointed Sevier a brigadier general. Apparently Sevier wanted to abandon the statehood concept and remain loyal to North Carolina, but the vast majority of the frontiersmen preferred otherwise. When the governor of North Carolina received word that Franklin leaders were continuing to conduct affairs as though they were a sovereign state and contended that it was their "duty" and inalienable right" to form "an

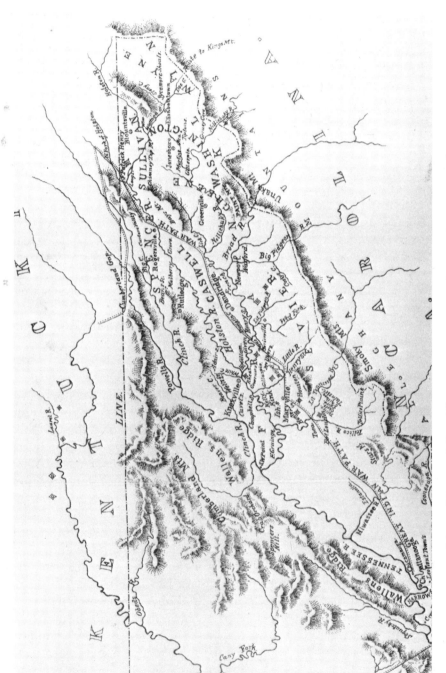

Map of State of Franklin. *From James R. Gilmore, John Sevier: The Commonwealth Builder (1887).*

independent state," he issued a manifesto stating that North Carolina would regain sovereignty over the revolting territory or "render it not worth possessing."

Attempts at conciliation divided the Franklin people into two warring factions. Sevier's fellow Washington countian, John Tipton, led a minority group and urged abandonment of the independence movement and reconciliation with the mother state. Sevier, however, urged on by the majority faction, took a stand against Tipton, and border warfare developed. Several were killed and wounded, and two of Sevier's sons were captured and held.

Sevier's term as governor of the State of Franklin expired in the spring of 1788, and for all practical purposes the abortive state came to an end. Sevier was arrested by Tipton on charges of treason, but was never tried. Within less than a year he had taken an oath of allegiance to North Carolina and was elected to the state senate. A few months later he was restored to his rank of brigadier general of the North Carolina militia.

The following year (November, 1789), North Carolina again ceded its western lands to the central government, and six months later President George Washington signed into law a measure for the government of the region, soon to be called the "Southwest Territory." The territory at the time consisted of two pockets of settlement separated by about 100 miles of wilderness; the eastern valley counties had a population of about 28,000, and the Cumberland settlements around Nashborough had about one-fourth that number. Sevier probably was the choice of a majority of the Western people for the position of Territorial Governor, but President Washington appointed William Blount instead.

Shortly before the government was formed, Sevier was elected to congress from North Carolina's western district, but retired after one term to become active in the territorial government. The Continental Congress had provided in the Ordinance of 1787 that the legislature of a territory should consist of a house of representatives and a "Legislative Council." The council was to consist of five men chosen from a slate of 10 prepared by the house. Representatives were elected in October of 1793 and assembled in February of 1794 to nominate the 10 men whose names were to be submitted to congress. Sevier was among the ten chosen, and ultimately he became one of the five selected by congress to form the council. The legislature assembled in August, 1794, and Sevier played an active role in preparing and enacting legislation. A major topic for conversation among the lawmakers was that of statehood, and Sevier was among those who the following year urged Governor Blount to reconvene the assembly to consider steps necessary for the formation of a state government. After Blount conferred with national leaders about procedure, he called the legislature into special session in August of 1795 to make plans for statehood. A census soon was taken to determine whether the territory had the legally prescribed 60,000 people, and, when the population proved to be well in excess of that figure, a constitutional convention was called to prepare fundamental law for the new state.

Along with these civic duties, Sevier also found time to lead assaults against the Cherokees and to speculate in land. His last major campaign against the Indians was in the summer and fall of 1793. The policy of the federal government had been that of attempting to protect both Indians and frontier whites from each other—something rendered exceedingly difficult because of the tremendous increase of whites who daily traversed the mountains to take up lands on the frontier. The Cherokees, fearing that continued encroachments by whites eventually would exterminate or drive them from their native soil, began hostilities on a large scale late in 1792. Blount, attempting to carry out federal policy, urged moderation. Finally, in the summer of 1793, Daniel Smith, Territorial Secretary who acted as governor when Blount was away, ordered an expedition against Cherokee towns during one of the governor's missions to Philadelphia. Sevier organized some 600 or 700 men to march against the Indians. Successful as usual, Sevier destroyed the Indian village of Etowah and brought to a close the aggressive activity of the Cherokees. The Knoxville *Gazette* hailed the work of "this experienced and valuable officer," and the people upon his return received him with adulation.

Most frontier leaders accumulated land, and Sevier was no exception. Not long after the Revolutionary War ended, Sevier began to accumulate thousands of acres in the eastern section, and, in July and August of 1788 received grants of more than 4,000 acres "in our Middle District"—along the Duck and Buffalo rivers. In 1795 he received 63,000 acres in Sumner County on the Cumberland River, and in the same year got 3,000 acres in Greene County. Earlier he had purchased 128,000 acres in East Tennessee in partnership with Landon Carter. Carl Driver, Sevier's chief biographer, has written that Nolichucky Jack, like most frontier leaders, well fit the description of "a frontier land gambler."

Sevier was married twice. His first wife, Sarah Hawkins (1746-1780), bore him 10 children (Joseph, James, John, Valentine, Richard, Elizabeth, Sarah, Mary Ann, Rebecca, and Nancy). She was born in Virginia, the daughter of Joseph and Sarah Marlin Hawkins, and was 15 when she was married. She died at the Nolichucky fort in Washington County and was buried in an unmarked grave near the fort. Not long after her death, Sevier married Catherine Sherrill (1754-1836), whom he had rescued four years earlier from the Cherokees during a surprise attack. They reared eight children (Catherine, Geoge Washington, Ruth, Joanne Goade, Samuel, Polly, Eliza, and Robert). She was born in North Carolina but came to the frontier settlements as a young girl with her parents. She lived most of her life in Tennessee but returned to Alabama a few months prior to her death to join members of her family. Buried at Russellville, her body was removed in 1922 and reinterred beside that of her husband on the court lawn in Knoxville. Although not active in formal church affairs, Sevier early in life expressed a preference for the Baptist church; on one occasion he gave three acres of land in Virginia on which a Baptist church was built. But his civil and military activities, along with his family and his landholdings, were the center of his life.

Delegates to the Constitutional Convention of 1796 prepared a constitution within a few weeks in January of that year and hastily dispatched a copy of it, along with a petition for admission to the Union, to President George Washington. On April 8 the president forwarded the documents to congress, along with a presidential message. Among the "privileges, benefits, and advantages" congress had conferred upon the Southwest Territory at the time of its creation, Washington said, was "the right of forming a permanent constitution and State Government, and of admission as a state . . . on an equal footing with the original States. . . ." After several weeks of debate, sometimes acrimonious, congress voted for admission, and President Washington signed the statehood bill on June 1, 1796, thus creating Tennessee as the 16th state.

In the meantime, Sevier has assumed the office of governor. The constitution had provided for a chief executive who would hold office for a two-year term and who could not serve for more than three consecutive terms. Sevier and a legislature had been elected in February, and the General Assembly convened on March 28, 1797. Legislators the following day, proclaimed that "Citizen John Sevier" had been "duly and constitutionally elected" governor of the state. On March 30, Sevier was inaugurated. In a brief address, he expressed gratitude for the confidence reposed in him and promised "to labor to discharge with fidelity" the duties of his office. Busy legislators chose Blount and William Cocke as United State Senators, divided the state into two congressional districts, divided old Tennessee County into Robertson and Montgomery counties, and enacted other legislation. The United States Senate later refused to accept Bount and Cocke until they had been elected by the legislature of "the State of Tennessee" and not of the "Southwest Territory." Consequently, Sevier was forced to call the lawmakers into extra session on July 30 for the purposes of electing two senators, providing for the election of a congressman, and selecting three presidential electors. Blount and Cocke were chosen over negligible opposition, and Andrew Jackson was elected later that year as the congressman.

Sevier served as governor for six terms, which was as long a period of time in the executive chair as anyone else in the history of the state served, although his first term was only 18 months because of a constitutional provision that the first governor should hold office only until the fourth Tuesday in September of 1797. He was reelected in 1797 without opposition, and in 1799 over only negligible opposition in Hawkins County by Judge Joseph Anderson and General John Conway. Constitutionally barred from seeking election in 1801, he returned to defeat incumbent Governor Archibald Roane by a two-to-one majority in 1803. He again defeated Roane by about the same majority in 1805, and then was elected to another term without opposition in 1807.

Many changes took place in the state while Sevier was governor. Perhaps the most important was the tremendous increase in population occasioned by the westward movement of settlers, who continued to pour in from North Carolina, Virginia, Pennsylvania, and other seaboard states. From a population of about 85,000 in 1796, the state increased to nearly 250,000 in 1809 when Sevier's final gubernatorial term ended. The section of the state now known as West Tennessee was in the hands of the Chickasaws and not settled by whites during Sevier's terms, but by 1809 most of Middle Tennessee (then called the "Western District") and most of the eastern division (except for an area in the southeast around present-day Chattanooga) had been cleared of Indian claims. More than 60 percent of the people lived in the central section as contrasted with only 30 percent when Sevier became governor.

Although the office of governor was by no means a "full-time" position comparable to that of the modern governor, still Sevier had problems which the foibles of human nature were sure to create. As significant and troublesome as any were the jealousies of prominent men associated with the attainment of rank in the state militia. All free men between the ages of 18 and 50 were subject to military duty, and they elected their field officers—a colonel and two majors in each county. Field officers of a military district (several counties grouped together) elected a brigadier general, and the field officers of the state elected their commanding general. Active members of militia companies elected their own officers below the rank of major. The governor issued commissions to all officers duly elected, but determining who had been legally chosen proved a vexatious problem for Sevier. To serve as an election judge was sure to make enemies and to take considerable time in gathering evidence where claims of fraud developed. Bitter disputes arose in Davidson, Sumner, Knox, and Washington counties, for example, and Sevier in desperation referred these to the legislature. Apparently the governor handled such matters as judiciously as he could under the circumstances, but he frequently was accused of political favoritism and of exerting gubernatorial influence to procure the selection of his friends and favorites.

Indian affairs was another matter which demanded much of the governor's attention. The question as to the exact location of the line distinguishing Indian and white lands as prescribed in the Holston Treaty of 1791 caused considerable unrest among both

Indians and whites, especially after federal authorities undertook a
strict enforcement of the treaty. When United States troops forcibly
removed some families from Indian lands and arrested others for
hunting game on the property, frontiersmen were ready to fight.
Sevier complained before the legislature and urged the lawmakers,
"by remonstrance or such other mode," to lay before the federal
government the rights and demands of white settlers. At the
same time, he said, legislators should "take measure to prevent
the encroachments of the Indians" upon lands purchased by
Tennesseans.

Other problems which Sevier faced during his first few years as
governor were associated with the disposition of Tennessee lands
which North Carolina had granted its Revolutionary soldiers,
internal improvements which included a road across the mountains into North Carolina, alleged land frauds which resulted in the
conviction and removal from office of a North Carolina Secretary
of State, and disagreements with Andrew Jackson.

As significant as anything else—and probably producing about
as much interest among the people—was the mounting animosity
between Sevier and Jackson, which resulted in a challenge to a duel.
Jackson had settled in Nashville not long after permanent settlements were made in the Cumberland territory, and soon rose to
political prominence. By 1801, when Sevier's third term as governor expired, Jackson had served briefly in both the United States
House of Representatives and Senate and had become a judge of
the court of law and equity in Tennessee. Ambitious politically,
Jackson attempted to assume direction of the Blount faction of the
state's chief political party after the Territorial governor died in
1800, and exerted considerable influence over Archibald Roane,
who was elected in 1801 to succeed Sevier as governor. Soon after
Roane was inaugurated, Major General Conway died, and Jackson,
desiring the prestige and influence which accompanied high military rank, moved forward to attempt to win the highest military
position in the state.

Sevier for years had considered himself the ranking Tennessean in military affairs, especially after his victory at King's Mountain and his many Indian battles, and he refused to permit
Jackson's attempt to gain the position of commanding general of

the Tennessee militia to go unchallenged. Therefore, as the field officers of the state prepared to select Conway's successor, they found that they had to choose from among Sevier, Jackson, and James Winchester of Sumner County. After the votes were counted, it was discovered that Sevier and Jackson each had received 17 and Winchester three. Sevier, confident that he would receive the support of at least two of the three who had voted for Winchester, urged that another ballot be taken; Jackson, however, confident of the support of Roane, demanded that the governor cast the deciding vote, as directed by law. Jackson was elected, but it was a hollow victory in that animosity between him and Sevier became magnified and Sevier gained as he declined in stature.

Sevier, eligible again for the governorship in 1803, prepared to dislodge the incumbent in the election scheduled for August of that year. In July, however, Jackson, seeking to aid Roane, published in a Nashville newspaper a lengthy assault upon Sevier, charging that he had forged 165 warrants for 640 acres of land each and that he had bribed the Secretary of State of North Carolina in order to have the warrants issued. Sevier effectively answered the charge, however, and went on to win election by a substantial majority.

Sevier was inaugurated on September 23, 1803, and scarely a week has elapsed when the feud with Jackson was reopened. After a chance meeting on the streets of Knoxville in which both berated the other and boasted of their services to the state, Jackson proposed a duel. Sevier, however, aware that dueling was illegal in the Volunteer State, informed Jackson of the law:

> I have some regard for the laws of the State over which I have the honor to preside [he wrote], although you, a Judge, appear to have none. It is hoped that if by any strange and unexpected event you should ever be metamorphosed into an upright and virtuous Judge, you will feel the propriety of being governed and guided by the laws of the State you are sacredly bound to obey and regard.

Jackson's popularity declined after his altercation with Sevier, and he became embroiled in a half dozen duels and brawls during the next decade; indeed, his popularity mounted only after his spectacular victory over the British at New Orleans. Sevier, however, increased in stature. He defeated challenger Archibald Roane in

1805 by a two-to-one vote, and was elected for a sixth and final term in 1807 over token opposition. In March of 1809, a few months before his term expired, he was nominated for a six-year term in the United States Senate but was defeated by Joseph Anderson by a vote of 23 to 16. In August, Knox Countians elected him without opposition to the state senate, and two years later he was elected to congress from the East Tennessee district. He was reelected in 1813 and 1815, but died on September 24, 1815, while on a mission in the Alabama territory where he had gone with United States troops to determine the Creek boundary. He was buried on the east bank of the Tallapoosa River near Fort Decatur after a military funeral.

Sevier was a true product of the frontier and was a hero in the Cincinnatus tradition. Effective as a legislator and an administrator, he was equally successful as a soldier. Blunt and direct, he was a true leader of men. Legislators, upon his retirement as governor in 1809, paid tribute to the "various and important services" he had rendered in his "civil and military capacity." Those services evidenced "an extent and a purity of patriotism which have justly secured to you the confidence of your fellow-citizens," legislators concluded. When in 1887 Sevier's body was disinterred and buried on the courthouse lawn in Knoxville, a monument was erected whose inscription well described his life's work:

> "John Sevier, Pioneer, soldier, statesman, and one of the founders of the Republic; Governor of the State of Franklin; six times Governor of Tennessee; four times elected to Congress; a typical pioneer, who conquered the wilderness and fashioned the State; a projector and hero of King's Mountain; fought thirty-five battles, won thirty-five victories; his Indian war cry 'Here they are! Come on boys!' "

SUGGESTED READINGS

Nearly a half century old and encumbered with a few errors, Carl Driver's *John Sevier: Pioneer of the Old Southwest* (Nashville, 1932) remains the definitive work on Nolichucky Jack. Robert H. White's *Messages of the Governors of Tennessee, 1796-1821,* Volume I, (Nashville, 1952) contains much material helpful in understanding the man and his times, as also does Cora Bales Sevier's and Nancy S. Madden's *Sevier Family History* (Washington, D.C., 1961). Samuel Cole Williams' *History of the Lost State of Franklin* (Johnson City, 1924) is the best description of that ill-fated venture, and Max Dixon in his *The Wataugans* (Nashville, 1976) writes well of Sevier and the people with whom he worked, fought, and lived.

3

NANCY WARD
by Ilene J. Cornwell

*N*ancy *(Nanye'*-hi) Ward, the last Beloved Woman of the Cherokee Indians, was much more than a "sufficient measure of civilization" during the middle 18th and early 19th centuries in the Territory Southwest of the River Ohio. She personified the courage and spirit of all the frontier men and women who sought peace and reconciliation during the turbulent, war-torn settlement years between 1755 and 1820.

In this century, Nancy Ward's life has been so highly romanticized that it is difficult to separate fact from fiction and legend. Historians have discovered, however, that she was born sometime in 1738. Her mother, Tame Doe, was a sister of Attakullakulla, civil chief of the Overhill Cherokees, who was becoming an influential leader about the time of Nancy's birth. Little is known of her father, but it has been theorized that he came from the Delaware tribe and by marriage joined the Wolf clan of the Cherokees. The baby at birth was given the name *Nanye' hi*, a tribal name meaning "spirit people." Ben Harris McClary, a widely known expert on Nancy Ward, stated that she was given the nickname *Isistu-na-gis-ka*, meaning Cherokee Rose or Wild Rose. The fine texture of Nancy's skin was compared to the velvety smoothness of the petals of the Wild Rose, which her people loved and cultivated throughout the region, and the nickname was bestowed upon her with pride and affection.

Nancy is not recorded in historical times until the early 1750s, when she became the wife of Kingfisher of the Deer clan. Shortly thereafter, she was catapulted to prominence and remained there until her death in 1820 (although some accounts say 1822).

In 1755, Nancy, already the mother of two children, accompanied her husband, Kingfisher, to what is now Georgia, and there her tribe engaged in battle their neighbors to the south, the Creeks, who were traditional enemies of the Cherokees. During the Battle of Taliwa, near Canton, Nancy "lay behind a log, chewing lead bullets to make [Kingfisher's] rifle fire more deadly." When Kingfisher was shot and killed, Nancy took up his weapon and his place, continuing the fight. Her effort is credited with inspiring the Cherokees to greater strength in battle, and Nancy led her people to ultimate victory over the Creeks.

In Chote, the Cherokee capital on the Little Tennessee River, stories of Nancy's valor spread among the clans. Her acclaim prompted the choosing of Nancy to fill the vacant position of *Aqi-qa-u-e,* or Beloved Woman, of the Cherokees. It was believed by the Cherokees that the Great Being spoke to them through the mouth of the Beloved Woman. In that position, she served as head of the Women's Council, which was made up of representatives from each clan. The role of Beloved Woman was most honored in the strongly matriarchial society of the Cherokees. She also was accorded a voice in the Council of Chiefs, where her words carried great weight, although her counsel was not always heeded. She often arbitrated between the factions advocating war and those desiring peace.

Nancy's position must have been most difficult to assume in the middle 1700s. The Cherokees were caught in a literal tug-of-war between France and England, and the task of trying to avoid confrontations with either power, while still promoting the well being of the populous Cherokee nation, called for both wisdom and strength—qualities not usually found in one as young as Nancy Ward when she was elevated to Beloved Woman. It seems reasonable to assume that her uncle, Attakullakulla, exerted considerable influence on her actions and philosophy during those fledgling years, and probably throughout the ensuing years until his death.

Attakullakulla, also known as Little Carpenter, was probably born between 1700 and 1712, according to historian James C. Kelly, on the Big Island of the French Broad River. He was, however, "a child of the Overhill Towns" which lay along the banks of the Little Tennessee and Hiwassie rivers. He was the son of an important family and one of the seven Cherokees who accompanied

Chattanooga artist Ben Hampton depicted Nancy Ward and her times in this unusual painting. A reproduction was presented to the Tennessee Historical Commission in 1977 and now hangs in the Commission's offices in Nashville. *Photograph courtesy the State Library and Archives.*

Sir Alexander Cuming to London in 1730 to pay homage to King
George. Little more was heard of him until 1736, when the French
sent emissaries into the Overhills, and Attakullakulla helped persuade his people to remain loyal to the English.

Historical perspective reveals Attakullakulla as the supreme
diplomatist of the native Americans in the middle 1700s. He sur-
reptitiously placated both the English and French to avoid "taking
sides," desiring only to improve trade relations with both factions
and thereby promote the interests of the Cherokees. It was, however, no easy task. His people often turned against him, and he was
viewed as a lackey of the British. Standing Turkey, who became in
1759 the *Chota Uka,* or "Beloved Man of Chota," took a strong
anti-British stand and was constantly at odds with Attakullakulla.
Although these two men often shared the reins of power, the tide of
popularity was fickle—never constant for either of them. Attakullakulla's influence with his people continually waxed and waned,
depending on fluctuating trade conditions and whether the French
or the English held the upper hand in the western frontier.

In the fall of 1759, the English garrison at Fort Loudoun—
built in 1757 by South Carolina in an effort to undergird England's
position in the area—found itself under siege by the Cherokees.
Greater French influence, coupled with abuses of the Cherokees by
Virginia and South Carolina, drew the Indians' loyalty away from
England and provoked hostilities. Attakullakulla, who had been
instrumental in securing the fort's location and construction, argued against attacking the English. His words were not heeded. He
moved into the fort in 1760 and lengthened the siege by having
Cherokee women slip "pumpkins and Fowles, corn and hogs into
the fort." This tactic worked only a short time and, by June, Attakullakulla could foresee approaching doom; he withdrew from
the fort. In August, Fort Loudoun surrendered. The terms of the
surrender stated that the fort's occupants would be allowed to
march either to Virginia or South Carolina with a Cherokee escort.
After the escort left the party at Cane Creek, a tributary of the
Tellico River, the whites were attacked by a strong force of
Cherokees who refused to acknowledge the treaty terms. The party
was almost totally massacred, with only a few men taken prisoners.
Appalled by the bloodshed, Attakullakulla voiced the hope "that he

might see the hot-headed people of his Nation well beaten and humbled."

Nancy Ward must have also been greatly disturbed by the actions for a number of reasons. After the completion of the fort in 1757, several traders established quarters within the walls of Fort Loudoun, and a few took Indian wives. One such trader was Bryant Ward, who married Nancy in the late 1750s. From her union with Ward was born a daughter, Elizabeth; she joined Nancy's household, which included the children, Catharine and Fivekiller, by Kingfisher. Elizabeth in early womanhood became the wife of Joseph Martin, North Carolina's agent to the Cherokee nation. This couple would also have significant influence in the affairs of the Cherokees. Ward, however, did not permanently settle among the tribe. Prior to 1760, he returned to his white family and home-place in South Carolina.

Two years after the outbreak of hostilities at Fort Loudoun, during which there were subsequent reprisals by the English, Attakullakulla traveled to Charleston, South Carolina, to negotiate a peace treaty. The Treaty of Charleston was ratified by the Cherokees in December 1761, and a truce was established between the two peoples.

The Royal Proclamation of 1763 forbade the settlers' movement farther west into the Cherokee country, but the pioneers chose to ignore the proclamation. The Watauga and Holston River valleys received an influx of settlers over the next five years and, by 1769, thickly populated settlements were encroaching upon Indian land. Attakullakulla, protesting the continued westward expansion, complained that his people were being driven away from the sacred Long Island of the Holston and that "guns were rattling" in the Holston hills.

The Treaty of Lochaber in 1770 ceded Cherokee land between the Kanawha and Holston rivers to the English for settlement, and by 1772 there were about 70 families settled along the Watauga River. Since the Royal Proclamation prohibited purchase of the Indians' land, the Wataugans reached an agreement with Attakullakulla to lease the land on which they were homesteading. As in the past, the Cherokee leader found himself caught between his concern for his people and the greed of the land-hungry pioneers.

He observed in 1772 that "The Great Being above is very good and provides for everybody. . . . He gave us this land, but the white people seem to want to drive us from it."

Unfortunately there is no record of Nancy Ward's attitude toward white encroachment during those crucial years. In 1772, when she was 35 years of age, she was visited at her lodge in Chote by Commissioner James Robertson of Watauga (he would much later be known as the "Father of Middle Tennessee" and the "Founder of Nashville," and would serve as government agent to the Cherokee nation). Robertson's papers include a description of Nancy's lodge with appointments of "barbaric splendor," and he regarded the Beloved Woman as "queenly and commanding." He did not, however, record their conversation or the reason for his visit to her.

In 1774, the Transylvania Company was organized by Judge Richard Henderson of North Carolina, and he approached the Cherokees to sell (illegally, by terms of the Royal Proclamation) more than 20 million acres of land; the area included the fertile soil of present-day Middle Tennessee and Central Kentucky. When Attakullakulla traveled to North Carolina to visit Henderson and inspect the goods for payment, he was accompanied by another Indian man and woman; although history does not provide their names, perhaps the woman was Nancy Ward, who traveled with her aged uncle.

The Transylvania or Watauga Purchase—also called the Sycamore Shoals Treaty—took place on March 17, 1775, and has been called the largest private or corporate real estate transaction in American history. The Transylvania Company purchased 20 million acres of land from the Cherokee Indians for 2,000 pounds sterling and goods worth 8,000 pounds sterling. Twelve-hundred Indians reputedly spent weeks in counsel at Sycamore Shoals prior to the signing of the deed. Chief Dragging Canoe, who is said to have been Attakullakulla's son, was adamantly opposed to selling land to the whites, but the other chiefs ignored his warnings and signed the deeds amidst great ceremony and celebration.

And what of Nancy Ward? Did she agree or disagree with the decision to sell Cherokee land? Her opinion is not recorded, but Attakullakulla's influence on her probably led her to adopt a philosophy similar to his: the white took what they wanted, so why not sell the land before it was taken? One can only guess at motivating thoughts and feelings.

Nancy Ward's position was similar to that of her uncle: she was caught in the "cross-fire" of doing what was best for her people, but at the same time trying to placate the English and the French forces. She, too, was often viewed by her people as a lackey of the British. Later she was viewed as a traitor to her own people.

As Beloved Woman of the Cherokees, it was Nancy's duty and privilege to prepare the sacred "Black Drink," an emetic of holly tea, before the warriors prepared for the warpath. For this reason, she was also called the "War Woman." She knew the details of any approaching attack, for she was a member of the council which decided for or against war, and this advantage allowed her to warn the settlers of impending attacks by her people.

In July 1776, Nancy Ward told Isaac Thomas of an approaching attack on the Watauga settlement, and helped him and two others escape from Chote. Several days later, her warning via Thomas reached John Sevier at Fort Watauga. Those in the fort, with adequate time to fortify the station, managed to withstand for more than two weeks a siege imposed by Dragging Canoe and Old Abram.

All of the fort's inhabitants, however, did not escape the Cherokees' wrath. Lydia Bean, wife of William Bean, who is said to have been Tennessee's "first permanent settler," was captured before she could reach the safety of the stockade. The Cherokees condemned her to death by fire, and she was taken to Toquo and tied to a stake at the top of a huge ceremonial mound. Nancy Ward arrived at the scene and reportedly declared, "No woman shall be burned at the stake while I am Beloved Woman!"

Mrs. Bean was spared and Nancy took her to Chote as her guest. During the time Lydia Bean resided at Chote, she imparted a good deal of knowledge to Nancy Ward concerning the white settlers' customs. From her Nancy learned the art of making butter and cheese from the milk of "the white man's buffalo" (cows). Later, Nancy would purchase cows and introduce dairying into the Cherokee nation.

In 1778 the death of Attakullakulla thrust Nancy into the role of arbitrator and primary peace-keeper between the Cherokee and white peoples. She had watched during the last three years of At-takullakulla's life as hostilities between the English and fron-tiersmen increasingly embroiled the Cherokees. Rejection by Dragging Canoe and his followers of the Watauga Purchase was quickly fanned to hatred of all settlers and prompted that faction to pledge loyalty to the Crown shortly after the outbreak of the American Revolution. Within a short time, that allegiance was compromised when a delegation of Mohawks, Ottowas, Nanatas, Delawares, Shawnees, and others came to Chote to entreat the Cherokees to resume the war (waged in 1774) against the whites. The representatives of the tribes warned the Cherokees that they would suffer reprisals from their red brothers if they refused to join in the attack against the settlers. Many of the leaders, such as Dragging Canoe and Old Abram, were anxious to drive the whites from the country, and the summer of 1776 was ablaze with battle. Other Cherokee leaders, like Attakullakulla and Nancy Ward, found themselves caught in the three-way struggle involving the warring tribes, the English, and the frontiersmen. Dividing lines between the battling factions became increasingly confused to the peace-seeking Cherokees. American forces from Virginia, North Carolina, and South Carolina struck with devastating power to destroy the Indian allies of England, and Attakullakulla, the year before his death, met with 85 other chiefs and Colonel William Christian of Virginia to negotiate peace. Dragging Canoe refused to treat for peace. Rather than accept terms agreed upon by the elder chiefs, he and his followers fled to Chickamauga, where they continued to wage war against the whites.

In 1780 the engagement of the Watauga men in battle with the English at King's Mountain, South Carolina, prompted the Cherokees to attempt to eliminate the small number of whites left to defend their homes. As she had previously done, Nancy Ward told Isaac Thomas of the impending attack and sent him to warn the Wataugans. John Sevier and his men had just returned home from the victorious battle at King's Mountain (later described by historians as the turning point of the Revolution in the South) and, acting on Nancy's warning, started toward Chote to intercept the warring Cherokees. The frontiersmen, hoping to destroy the "heart and strength" of the Cherokee nation, obliterated Chote. Nancy Ward and her family were taken into protective custody, but she left the whites the next year and returned to Chote to help rebuild the Cherokee capital.

The Cherokees, except for the band led by Dragging Canoe at Chickamauga, had been crushed by the white onslaught and were ordered to appear before the frontiersmen in July of 1781 to enact a peace treaty. Nancy Ward, the first Indian woman to actively engage in treaty negotiations, was the featured speaker. She told the gathering in dramatic eloquence: "Our cry is for peace; let it continue. . . . This peace must last forever. Let your women's sons be ours; our sons be yours. Let your women hear our words."

Response to her words was made by Colonel William Christian, who said, "Mother: We have listened well to your talk . . . . No man can hear it without being moved by it. . . . Our women shall hear your words. . . . We will not meddle with your people if they will be still and quiet at home and let us live in peace."

Following this Treaty of Long Island, the majority of the Cherokees did, indeed, remain "still and quiet at home." But not the war chief, Dragging Canoe, and his Chickamaugans, who continued ferociously to oppose white settlement. The years between 1781 and 1792, when Dragging Canoe died, were filled with bloodshed and violence.

There apparently was little that Nancy could do to dissuade the warring Cherokee element. Although Dragging Canoe and his staunch supporters and brothers, Little Owl and The Badger, were Nancy's first cousins, they did not share her philosophy of peaceful co-existence.

The last record of Nancy actually saving the lives of white settlers by intervening on their behalf was in 1783. Two traders had gone among the Cherokees with weapons hidden in their possessions; the Indians considered the act one of aggression and would have killed the men, but Nancy interceded and the trade agreement was concluded without mishap.

At the Treaty of Hopewell, in South Carolina in 1785, Nancy Ward again made a moving plea for peace. "I am fond of hearing that there is a peace," she said, "and I hope you have now taken us by the hand in real friendship." At the conclusion of her address to the commissioners, she presented to them a string of beads, symbolic of a "chain of friendship," saying, "We hope the chain of friendship will never more be broken."

Nancy at that time was 47 years old and, for the next thirty years or so, would spend her life in relative obscurity. She remained at Chote, offering shelter to many homeless and orphaned children, and watched as her daughters, Catharine, who had married John Walker, and Elizabeth, who had married Indian agent Joseph Martin, gave her grandchildren. She continued to hold the position of Beloved Woman, but times were changing for the Cherokee nation, and Nancy Ward had to change with the times.

Ben Harris McClary summed up the situation when he wrote, ". . . The Cherokees were learning the ways of the settlers, now so geographically close to them. They were becoming farmers and cattle-raisers and in some instances were developing a culture of their own, yet in a likeness of the white man's. Government too was changing; the old system of clan-tribal loyalty was giving way to demands for a republican form of government."

The last Council meeting was held in 1817, and Nancy, then ill and too old to attend, "sent her distinctive walking cane to represent her." She approved the new form of government, but sent a written message asking the leaders to retain what was left of their Cherokee lands. Her wish was repected only a few years; the Hiwassee Purchase of 1819 deeded to the whites all Cherokee land north of the Hiwassee River—including Chote.

Nancy Ward and her family of waifs moved to a new home close to the Ocoee River, near the present town of Benton. She reportedly operated an inn for travelers and, when she died, was buried on a hill nearby. Her son, Fivekiller, and brother, Longfellow, had moved to homeplaces near Nancy Ward's, and she was buried between those two who had predeceased her.

Ben Harris McClary gave a graphic account of her death: "When she died, so her great-grandson reported in sworn testimony, a light rose from her body, fluttered like a bird around the room, and finally flew out the door. It was watched by the startled people in attendance until it disappeared, moving in the direction of Chote. Thus Nancy Ward passed from life into legend."

And Nancy's life is tangled in legend, but she was, in fact, an

James Abraham Walker, believed to have been a descendant of Nancy Ward, created this tombstone sculpture of Nancy in the early 1900s. He apparently hoped to place it on her grave, but circumstances prevented it, and the statue stands today in the small Arnwine Cemetery overlooking the Clinch River near Liberty Hill, Tennessee. *Photograph courtesy the Tennessee Historical Commission; original furnished by John Rice Irwin, Museum of Appalachia in Norris, Tennessee.*

exceptional leader of the Cherokees for almost 50 years. Her desire and efforts for peaceful co-existence with the whites placed her far above the "sufficient measure of civilization" alluded to by Emerson, especially during the strife-torn years in the middle-to-late 1700s and the early 1800s in the Old Southwest. History might have unfolded in a far different manner if the Cherokees as a people had heeded the counsel of the Beloved Woman.

SUGGESTED READINGS

Although there are only a limited number of publications devoted solely to Nancy Ward, many of the published works dealing with settlement of the western frontier, or the Territory Southwest of the River Ohio, mention her in regard to her notable peace efforts and her influence in favor of limited "English cultivation" of the Cherokee way of life. The following three publications were particularly beneficial in preparing this chapter on Nancy Ward and her times:

"Nancy Ward: The Last Beloved Woman of the Cherokees," by Ben Harris McClary, *Tennessee Historical Quarterly*, XXI, 1962.

"Notable Persons in Cherokee History: Attakullakulla," by James C. Kelly, *Journal of Cherokee Studies*, III, 1978.

Nancy Ward-Dragging Canoe, by Pat Alderman, 1978.

Other publications, housed in the Tennessee State Library and in my private collection of historical works, which were helpful and which the reader may wish to consult for information on Nancy Ward and the settlement of Tennessee, include:

Annals of Tennessee, by J. G. M. Ramsey, Charleston, S.C., 1853.

The Civil and Political History of the State of Tennessee, by John Haywood, Knoxville, TN, 1823.

Early Travels in the Tennessee Country, 1540-1800, by Samuel Cole Williams, Johnson City, TN, 1928.

From Settlement to Statehood: A Pictorial History of Tennessee to 1796, by James C. Kelly, Nashville, TN, 1977.

History of the American Indian, by James Adair, London, England, 1775; edited by Samuel Cole Williams and reprinted by the National Society of Colonial Dames in America, 1930.

A History of Tennessee and Tennesseans, by Will T. Hale and Dixon L. Merritt, Vol. I, Chicago, Ill., 1913.

The Long Island of the Holston: Sacred Island of the Cherokee Nation, by Muriel M. C. Spoden, Nashville, TN, 1977.

Natural and Aboriginal History of Tennessee up to the First Settlement by White People in 1768, by John Haywood, Nashville, TN, 1823.

The Overmountain Men, by Pat Alderman, Johnson City, TN, 1970.

The Papers of Thomas Jefferson, edited by Julian P. Boyd, Vol. IV, Princeton, N.J., 1951.

Seedtime on the Cumberland, by Harriett Simpson Arnow, New York, N.Y., 1960.

The Tennessee, by Donald Davidson, Vol. I, New York, N.Y., 1946.

Tennessee During the American Revolutionary War, by Samuel Cole Williams, Nashville, TN, 1944.

Tennessee: The Dangerous Example, by Mary French Caldwell, Nashville, TN, 1974.

Tribes That Slumber, by Madeline Kneberg and Thomas M. N. Lewis, Knoxville, TN, 1958.

The Wataugans, by Max Dixon, Nashville, TN, 1976.

The Winning of the West, by Theodore Roosevelt, New York, N.Y., 1891-1896.

*   *   *

Special acknowledgement is offered for the consent to reproduce the photographs accompanying this chapter. All illustrations except those of Nancy Ward are from the private collection of Dr. James C. Kelly, Nashville, who is a noted authority on colonial history and early Indians of the Southeast. The tombstone statue of Nancy Ward was photographed by John Rice Irwin, owner and director of the Museum of Appalachia in Norris, Tennessee (he furnished the original print to the Tennessee Historical Commission in 1974 for use in the *Tennessee Blue Book, 1975-76*). Douglas Underwood, a photographer and the publisher of *The Westview* in Nashville, produced copies of the illustrations.

Andrew Jackson. *Courtesy National Portrait Gallery, Smithsonian Institution, Washington, D. C.*

4

ANDREW JACKSON
by Robert V. Remini

*P*erhaps more than any other man in American history, Andrew Jackson was the nation's finest image of itself. To the fullest degree, he personified the promise of American life, for he was the original "self-made man." Between the formidable obstacles he overcame to achieve this distinction and the magnitude of his accomplishments, he seemed to demonstrate through his life the truth of the propositions upon which this nation was founded. Orphaned at an early age, burdened by poverty and limited educational opportunities, he nonetheless distinguished himself as lawyer, planter, military commander, and public servant. Moreover, his success went beyond mere personal triumph. His achievements, both military and political, contributed substantially to the growth and vitality of the United States. For much of his life he served his country with rare devotion and dedication. He was a singular, complex, contradictory, and extraordinary man.

To a large extent, the enormous dimensions of his triumphs, as well as his success in overcoming personal handicaps, resulted from unique character flaws and strengths. He was a complex of driving ambition, strong loyalties, fierce hatreds, and rigid personal discipline. He combined qualities of steely determination, acute intelligence, and supreme self-confidence to win an overwhelming military victory at New Orleans in 1815 despite a near total lack of military training or experience. Later he led the nation as president through a period of significant political, economic, and intellectual change wihout any of the credentials of education and former public service normally required of candidates for the presidency. By his victory over the British, he restored the nation's confidence in itself to defend and preserve its liberty and independence. As president of the United States, he led the country as it haltingly entered the modern age.

Andrew Jackson's life bridged roughly the years from the American Revolution to the eve of the Civil War. His father, Andrew, and his mother, Elizabeth Hutchinson, migrated from Carrickfergus, Northern Ireland, in 1765 along with hundreds of other Scotch-Irish. They probably landed in Pennsylvania and slowly moved southward to the Waxhaw settlement, located along the boundary separating North and South Carolina, following a route taken earlier by other members of the family. Here they settled on new land adjacent to the Twelve Mile Creek, a branch of the Catawba River, and for two years struggled to improve the farm. Then suddenly the father died, and at approximately the same time Elizabeth Jackson gave birth to her third son—on March 15, 1767—and named him Andrew for his father.

Educated at an academy conducted by Dr. William Humphries and later at a school run by James Stephenson, young Andrew interrupted his studies with the outbreak of the American Revolution and rode with Colonel William Richardson Davie at the attack on the British post of Hanging Rock. His oldest brother, Hugh, died immediately after the Battle of Stono Ferry, and Andrew and his brother Robert fell into British hands shortly thereafter. Imprisoned at Camden, both boys contracted smallpox. Their mother arranged their release in exchange for British prisoners, and, although she pulled Andrew through his illness, Robert died almost immediately after their return home. While Andrew was still recovering, his mother journeyed to Charleston to nurse American prisoners of war held in prison ships. There she contracted cholera and died after a short illness.

A war-scarred veteran at the age of fourteen, Andrew lived with relatives for a time and drifted through a succession of occupations, including school teaching and assisting in a saddler's shop. In 1784 he decided to become a lawyer and moved to Salisbury, North Carolina, where he studied at the office of Spruce MacCay. After obtaining a license to practice but finding limited legal opportunities in the East, Jackson joined a group of fellow lawyers and migrated to Tennessee to serve as public prosecutor. He settled in

Nashville, built a successful law practice, and fell in love with Rachel Donelson, whose family numbered among the original settlers of Middle Tennessee. Rachel was already married to Lewis Robards of Kentucky, but had left him and returned to her mother's home. A divorce eventually was obtained but Andrew and Rachel married in Natchez in 1791 before this legal action had been completed. They repeated their vows on January 18, 1794, when the final divorce decree was granted.

As a capable and energetic young lawyer with ties to one of the most important families in Tennessee, Jackson rose quickly in politics. Allied with the political faction of William Blount, the territorial governor, Jackson was elected to the convention which wrote the constitution under which Tennessee was admitted in 1796 as a state in the Union. He was elected sole representative to the U.S. House of Representatives and subsequently to the U.S. Senate. He resigned from the Senate after serving one session and accepted election to the Tennessee Superior Court, where he sat on the bench for six years. While few of his decisions survive, an early biographer claimed that his opinions were "short, untechnical, unlearned, sometimes ungrammatical, and generally right."

To augment his income, Jackson pursued a number of business enterprises. He opened a store where he sold a variety of goods to settlers in the Cumberland district and as far away as Natchez. Over the years he formed several partnerships, the first with his brother-in-law, Samuel Donelson, and later with Thomas Watson, John Hutchings, and John Coffee. He also speculated in land, on one notable occasion in his dealings with David Allison nearly toppled into bankruptcy. Jackson finally settled at the Hermitage, just a short distance from Nashville, where in time he built an imposing mansion, raised cotton and foodstuffs, and bred racehorses.

When the war with Britain broke out in 1812, Jackson was the major general of the Tennessee Militia, elected to the position by the field officers of the militia. Despite his scant military training and experience, he quickly developed into an excellent general, indeed the best American general in the War of 1812. What made him so remarkable were his outstanding leadership qualities and a superhuman—almost demonic—determination to defeat the enemy and rescue the nation's honor. The loyalty and affection he won from the men who served under him was reflected in the nickname they gave him—"Old Hickory."

In 1813 Jackson and militia were sent against the Creek Indians in the South, who had used the opportunity of the war against Great Britain to attack the southern frontier. In a series of successful engagements, Jackson crushed the Creeks, imposed a punitive treaty that divested the Indians of millions of acres of land, and then hurried to New Orleans in time to repell a British invasion. There he inflicted a devastating defeat on the enemy, and his victory so elated the American people that they fashioned him into a popular hero for whom no honor or reward adequately expressed their gratitude and obligation.

Again, in 1818, he added further laurels to his military record by pursuing the Seminole Indians, who had been raiding the American frontier, into Spanish Florida and decisively defeating them. Then he wrested Florida from Spanish control. Although his actions precipitated an international crisis, complicated by his execution of two British subjects who aided the Indians, they ultimately led to the American purchase of Florida. In addition, they provided John Quincy Adams, the secretary of state, with the means to press for settlement of the western boundary of the Louisiana Territory. As a result, Spain agreed to recognize a line that extended to the Pacific Ocean, thus transforming the United States into a transcontinental power.

Jackson served as territorial governor of Florida for a few months, officiating at the transfer of ownership and establishing a civil administration under American auspices. His tenure was short and turbulent, but he provided Florida with an energetic and efficient government that smoothed the transition of an essentially foreign land into the American system. Just as important for Florida's future development was the caliber of men he attracted to the territory and to its political life.

Jackson's immense popularity with all classes of people in all sections of the country made him an obvious choice for president. In 1823 the Tennessee legislature not only elected him to the U.S. Senate but nominated him for the presidency. Although he won a popular and electoral plurality in the ensuing election of 1824, he did not receive the electoral majority required by the Constitution, for there were three active candidates in the race besides himself: John Quincy Adams, Henry Clay, and William H. Crawford. Consequently the election went to the House of Representatives where, after much political maneuvering, John Quincy Adams was elected president on the first ballot. Jackson resigned his Senate seat and returned home, convinced that a "corrupt bargain" between Adams and Clay had thwarted the popular will and wrongly deprived him of the presidency. He and his friends immediately began a campaign to win his election in 1828, and with the assistance of his Tennessee allies, Martin Van Buren of New York, John C. Calhoun of South Carolina, Thomas Hart Benton of Missouri, along with a reinvigorated political machine that subsequently called itself the Democratic Party, Jackson won a stunning popular and electoral victory over Adams in 1828 after a particularly vicious and sordid campaign. Then, at the moment of his great triumph, his wife Rachel died suddenly of a heart attack on December 23, 1828.

At the time, many people interpreted Jackson's electoral victory as a sign of the arrival of popular democracy in America. Historians later would exaggerate its meaning and speak of the "rise of the common man," as though ordinary citizens had finally hurtled all the obstacles blocking their way to full participation in the electoral process. Actually the common man had been rising for decades, yet the nation had a long way to go to achieve democracy for all its inhabitants.

Jackson served as president during a period in which the nation underwent enormous cultural, political, and economic changes, changes that inaugurated the emergence of modern America. And, in the minds of many, Jackson symbolized the nation during this transition. As president, he believed himself the true representative of all the people—and responsible to them. Later his name was associated with a brand of democracy that advocated equality of opportunity for all, a concept that each person had a right to pursue his individual goals unhampered by a central government awarding favors to a select few. Although Jackson was a conservative, Southern, landed slaveowner, he believed that government must make no distinctions between social and economic classes, but rather "shower its favors alike on the high and low, the rich and the poor. . . ." Moreover, it was a period in American history—sometimes call the Age of Jackson—when the popular will was extolled as wise and good and necessary to free government. It was a period which condemned privilege, deference, and elitism.

More than anything else, Jackson advanced the concept of the strong chief executive. He expanded presidential powers through his creative use of the veto and his leadership of Congress and the Democratic Party. He was the first president to veto legislation for reasons other than constitutional. He claimed the right to veto whatever the president deemed inimical to the best interests of the American people. Also, he was the first president to employ the pocket veto. By his masterful use of this constitutional power, Jackson seized for the president an active role in the legislative process and materially increased executive power.

Because he advocated limited government and opposed public works at federal expense, particularly when his political enemies benefitted, Jackson vetoed the Maysville Road bill, which proposed a stretch of the National Road to be constructed from Maysville to Lexington, Kentucky. He argued that the burden of paying for internal improvements belonged to the states.

Jackson also vetoed a bill to recharter the Second National Bank of the United States because he believed the Bank represented an ominous concentration of economic and political power. To Jackson's mind, the Bank was a monopoly with special privileges dedicated to the interests of the rich and powerful at the expense of the many. When the laws, said Jackson in his veto, "undertake to add . . . exclusive privileges, to make the rich richer and the potent more powerful, the humble members of society—the farmers, mechanics, and laborers—. . . have a right to complain of the injustice of their Government." Again and again he reminded the people that it was not in "splendid government" supported by monopolies and "aristocratical establishments" that they found their liberties protected, but in a plain system which granted favors to none but evenhandedly dispensed its blessings to all.

Early in his first administration, Jackson attempted to establish the principle of rotation of office. Governmental office was not created to give support to particular people at public expense, he said, nor did any man have an intrinsic right to official station. Offices were created solely for the benefit of the people, and, therefore, no one was wronged if removed because "neither appointment to nor continuance in office is a matter of right." He believed that all intelligent men could serve the government on a regular, rotating basis. Unfairly accused of inaugurating the "spoils system," Jackson neither introduced the system nor employed it extensively to reward his friends and supporters. He hoped his principle would encourage greater public participation in government which, in turn, would necessarily advance the democratization of American institutions.

In no other instance did Jackson more clearly demonstrate his conception of the Federal Union than in the dramatic conflict over the Tariff of 1832. Southern planters condemned high tariffs, which they regarded as unconstitutional and an unfair intrusion of government into the economic affairs of the major sections of the country. Thus when the Tariff of 1832 passed Congress and received Jackson's signature, South Carolina summoned a convention which nullified the tariff, forbade the collection of customs duties within the state, and warned the federal government that if coercion was attempted against it, the state would secede from the Union. In a brilliant exercise of presidential power, Jackson terminated the nullification controversy and prevented South Carolina's secession. Combining a willingness to compromise with a promise to punish treason, he avoided bloodshed and upheld the supremacy of federal law. A Compromise Tariff was passed in 1833, and South Carolina repealed its nullification.

Jackson's administration began the tragic history of Indian removal. He had long advocated physical removal of the Indian tribes to the western country beyond the Mississippi River. Although the idea did not originate with him, going back at least as far as President Jefferson, Jackson believed removal beneficial to both whites and Indians. At his suggestion, Congress passed the Indian Removal Act in 1830, by which lands held by Indians within the states were exchanged for lands west of the Mississippi. Then, in 1834, the Indian Territory was established in present-day Oklahoma in the hope that the Indians would find a secure refuge there from the white man. But the actual removal, most of which began after Jackson left the presidency, turned into a death march. The tribes were hurried along a "trail of tears," as the Cherokees called it, to lands they regarded as a desolate, treeless, waterless plain. The forceful, often treacherous, eviction of thousands of Indian families from their ancestral homes produced many deaths by hunger and disease during the westward trek. Although Jackson had always intended removal as a means of preserving Indian life and culture, the actual result nearly produced the exact opposite.

In his conduct of foreign affairs, Jackson pursued a vigorous, at times, aggressive policy. But his willingness to compromise at the appropriate moment averted armed conflict. He nearly provoked war with France over spoliation claims of American citizens for seizure of ships and cargoes during the Napoleonic Wars. As the two nations recognized their drift toward war, they indicated a willingness to compromise, and ultimately the French paid 25 million francs in settlement. Jackson also settled claims against Denmark and the Kingdom of Naples. The first United States treaty with an Asian nation was signed in 1833 when Siam agreed to American trade on the basis of a most favored nation. Of greater value and interest to the American people was Jackson's successful termination of the dispute with Britain over trade with the West Indies. After prolonged negotiations, United States and British West Indian ports were opened on terms of full reciprocity.

Jackson's hold on the affection and trust of the American people was so strong that at the end of his eight years in office he was able to determine the nomination and election of his successor, Martin Van Buren. At the inauguration of Van Buren, the people once more swarmed to Washington to honor Old Hickory. This time they did not shout or applaud. As the carriage conveying the two presidents moved down Pennsylvania Avenue, the spectators simply stared in almost absolute silence. Then, in a gesture of profound respect, the men in the crowd removed their hats as a salute to their hero. Thomas Hart Benton, senator from Missouri, commented: "For once the rising was eclipsed by the setting sun."

Jackson retired to the Hermitage in the spring of 1837. For the remainder of his life he took an active interest in national affairs. As an ardent expansionist, he favored the annexation of Texas and Oregon even at the risk of war. He delighted in the election to the presidency of his protege, James Knox Polk, in 1844, particularly since it meant the defeat of his long-time political enemy, Henry Clay, and the apparent acceptance by the American people of the Democratic platform pledging continued westward expansion. He died at the age of 78 on June 8, 1845, probably from a heart attack. He was buried next to his beloved wife in the garden adjacent to his home.

SUGGESTED READINGS

The biographies of Andrew Jackson include John Spencer Bassett, *The Life of Andrew Jackson* (New York, 1916); Marquis James, *The Life of Andrew Jackson* (Indianapolis and New York, 1938); James Parton, *Life of Andrew Jackson* (New York, 1866) and Robert V. Remini, *Andrew Jackson and the Course of American Empire,* 1767-1821 (New York, 1977).

Valuable monographs treating the Jacksonian era are Arthur M. Schlesinger, Jr., *The Age of Jackson* (Boston, 1946); Glyndon Van Deusen, *The Jacksonian Era* (New York, 1959); Edward Pessen, *Jacksonian American* (Homewood, Illinois, 1972) and Robert V. Remini, *The Revolutionary Age of Andrew Jackson,* (New York, 1976). Other useful monographs and biographies include: William W. Freehling, *Prelude to Civil War: The Nullification Controversy in South Carolina* (New York, 1965); Grant Foreman, *Indian Removal* (Norman, 1953); Bray Hammond, *Banks and Politics in America* (Princeton, 1957); Charles Wiltse, *John C. Calhoun* (New York, 1951); Irving Bartlett, *Daniel Webster* (New York, 1978); Robert V. Remini, *Andrew Jackson and the Bank War* (New York, 1969); Thomas Govan, *Nicholas Biddle* (Chicago, 1959); Samuel F. Bemis, *John Quincy Adams* (New York, 1961); Louis Filler, *The Crusade Against Slavery* (New York, 1960); William N. Chambers, *Old Bullion Benton* (Boston, 1956).

Brief biographies of the major figures of this period are: Gerald T. Capers, *John C. Calhoun, Opportunist* (Gainesville, 1962); Robert V. Remini, *Andrew Jackson* (New York, 1965); Clement Eaton, *Henry Clay* (Boston, 1955); and Richard Current, *Daniel Webster* (New York, 1956).

General histories for the early 19th century include: John R. Howe, *From the Revolution through the Age of Jackson* (Englewood Cliffs, N.J., 1973) and Raymond H. Robinson, *The Growing of America, 1789-1848* (Boston, 1973).

Sequoyah. *Photograph courtesy the State Library and Archives.*

5

SEQUOYAH
by Ronald N. Satz

No other Tennessean has been so honored by whites and Indians alike as Sequoyah, the inventor of the Cherokee syllabary. The exact date of Sequoyah's birth, like many other details of his life, is uncertain, but scholars have suggested either 1760 or 1770 as the most likely possibilities. Sequoyah's birthplace was the town of Tuskegee, near Fort Loudoun on the Tennessee River in the beautiful East Tennessee country; this was the home of the Overhill Cherokees. The settlements of the Overhill people constituted the most remote, independent, and dynamic region of the Cherokee tribe, whose numerous towns scattered among the southern Appalachian Mountains had a population of perhaps 22,000 in the early historic period.

Sequoyah's parentage has long been a subject of interest to biographers. White historians have focused their attention on ascertaining the identity of Sequoyah's father, who is generally conceded to have been a white man. Some writers maintain that George Gist, a German peddler whose travels brought him to the Overhill country, was Sequoyah's father. Other historians, including Samuel C. Williams, a former member of the Tennessee Supreme Court, have argued that a more likely condidate was Nathaniel Gist, the progenitor of a line of distinguished Americans and a friend of George Washington, who traveled among the Overhill Cherokees as a hunter, explorer, and soldier. Cherokee traditionalists, however, pay little attention to either argument. They point out that Sequoyah, regardless of the true identity of his father, was completely enculturated as a Cherokee Indian—he could neither read, write, nor speak English, and he did not look like a mixed blood. They also note that early Cherokee society was matrilineal and that Sequoyah was raised by his Cherokee mother, who was of the Red Paint clan.

While little is known about the details of Sequoyah's youth, the daily life of Cherokee boys was generally full of activity. In the spring they helped the men clear ground for crops. When the women and the girls took over the planting, the older boys were free to join the men in hunting and fishing. Because skill in hunting was essential for Cherokee men, the elders in each town arranged shooting matches for the boys. Oral tradition was important to the Cherokees, for they had no written language, and the youngsters listened attentively to the older men as they told and retold stories of their experiences as hunters and warriors. Sequoyah doubtless shared these experiences with other boys of his age. Unlike most of his peers, however, he apparently spent much time wandering about aimlessly in the forest in deep thought or carving objects from pieces of wood.

As a youth, Sequoyah exhibited great interest in the arts. Some writers maintain that his interest deepened after an illness, or perhaps after an accident suffered on a hunting trip, left him lame in one leg, but the exact date and nature of his affliction are uncertain. Although Sequoyah helped his mother with her farming chores and her fur trading activities, his interest in the arts never diminished. He painted pictures on bark, smooth wooden boards, and pieces of tanned deerskin whenever he had an opportunity, and he became a skilled silversmith.

Before the tide of white settlement engulfed the Overhill country in the early 1800s, Sequoyah joined other Tennessee Cherokees who moved south to Cherokee towns in Georgia and Alabama. He settled in Willstown in present-day DeKalb County, Alabama. There he conducted a fur trading business, continued his work as a silversmith, and began to labor as a blacksmith. His home quickly became a gathering place for Indians desiring his wares and seeking good conversation. Sequoyah apparently had a natural manual dexterity, a feeling for beauty, a keen eye for business, and a flair for discourse.

Some time about 1809, Sequoyah embarked on a quest that became the focus of his life for the next 12 years. Although there are various accounts of how it happened, scholars agree that Sequoyah became enchanted by the "talking leaves" (printed and written pages) of the white man. Although he could neither read, write, nor speak English and was totally ignorant of the workings of any alphabet, he vowed that he would create a writing system for his people. A friend had written what he thought Sequoyah's name sounded like in English on a "talking leaf" so that Sequoyah could make a punch and stamp his trademark on the fine silver pieces he made. Pondering over the symbols (which he could not read) that his friend had written, Sequoyah was intrigued by the curious lettering: "George Guess." Fascinated by the fact that "talking leaves" enabled a white person to know the thoughts of another, even if that person was many miles away, he was certain that a written language would be beneficial to his people as well. Smoking incessantly on his long-stemmed pipe, he began working on the development of a writing system. His efforts to harness the magic of the white man's "talking leaves" became a virtual obsession.

As Sequoyah labored arduously at his task during the next three years, the Cherokees were being drawn into the conflict between the United States and hostile Creek Indians during the War of 1812, which became known as the Creek War. A faction of the Creek Indians, ancient enemies of the Cherokees, had massacred the inhabitants of Fort Mims in what is today Alabama on August 30, 1813. The Cherokees earlier had rejected pleas of the Shawnee warrior Tecumseh, who urged them to join his Creek and British allies in a holy war against Americans. Anxious to win the respect and good will of the American government, the Cherokees fought as allies of the United States during the war.

Sequoyah enlisted on the side of the Americans on October 7, 1813. He served for three months as a private in a company of Mounted and Foot Cherokees, which formed a part of Cherokee Colonel Gideon Morgan's regiment of Cherokee warriors. During Sequoyah's period of service, some Cherokee warriors, wearing white feathers and deer's tails to distinguish themselves from the enemy, participated in an attack on the Creek town of Tallushatchee. On the morning of November 3, 1813, a thousand men, including white Tennessee volunteers and militia and some of their Indian allies, encircled Tallushatchee and systematically killed every warrior in the town. As Davy Crockett later admitted, "We shot them like dogs." Sequoyah's role in the fighting is unclear, but several authors include him among the combatants. When his term of service expired two months later, Sequoyah reenlisted. On March 27, 1814, his regiment aided General Andrew Jackson during the famous Battle of Horseshoe Bend, which inflicted a decisive defeat on the hostile Creeks.

Following the battle, Sequoyah returned to Willstown, married a Cherokee woman named Sally in accordance with "the laws, usages, and customs" of the Cherokees, and raised a family. More than ever before, however, his thoughts turned to creating a written language for his people. Perhaps his contact with American soldiers, who frequently received news from home via "talking leaves," played a role in encouraging him to resume his work in earnest.

Meanwhile, the events of the years following the War of 1812 greatly complicated the lives of the Cherokee people. General Jackson who, assisted by his Cherokee allies, had triumphed over the hostile Creeks during the war, now sought to secure land cessions not only from the Creeks but from *all* Southern tribes. In 1816 Sequoyah was among a group of Cherokee leaders who succumbed to the pressures exerted by Jackson and signed an unpopular treaty ceding a large section of their land in northwestern Alabama immediately south of the Tennessee River. A year later, in 1817, Jackson promised transportation by flatboats, weapons and ammunition, various equipment and supplies, and provisions for each Cherokee warrior who would enroll his family for emigration to what is today Arkansas. Sequoyah was one of many Cherokees who took advantage of this offer. In 1818 he joined other Cherokees who set out down the Tennessee River bound for Arkansas.

Cherokee Indians had settled in the Arkansas country as early as the 1780s when it was still owned by Spain. Following the Louisiana Purchase in 1803, when the area became an American possession, more and more eastern Cherokees went there to live. The majority of these settlers were traditionalists who longed to reestablish in that western wilderness the old Cherokee way of life, which was slowly dying in the East as a result of white influence. It was among these Cherokee people in present-day Pope County that Sequoyah settled. He quickly resumed his effort to formulate a written language as a contribution to the revitalization of Cherokee native culture.

Sequoyah's earliest efforts apparently were directed toward making individual signs for each Cherokee word. He made the various signs on bark, using a quill as a pen and pokeberry juice as ink. According to one account, he compared his work to "catching a wild animal and taming it." Eventually Sequoyah discovered that making signs for every word was too cumbersome a task. Then he decided upon a syllabary—a set of written characters, each one of which represented a syllable. The specific symbols of the final syllabary of 86 characters (one was later dropped) were modeled after English, Greek, and Hebrew letters. Because Sequoyah could not read any of the languages whose symbols he borrowed, he wrote some letters upside down and others sideways. Nevertheless, in 1821 his task of 12 years was over.

Eager to test his new invention, Sequoyah taught his little daughter Ahyoka the syllabary. She mastered it quickly. Then he informed his friends and neighbors in Arkansas of his success. Elated with his discovery and anxious to share it with tribal leaders in the East, Sequoyah returned to the Cherokee country in the southern Appalachian mountains. There he held a demonstration of his invention for skeptical members of the tribal council. Ahyoka read and answered a message that her father wrote using the syllabary. The news spread rapidly throughout the eastern Cherokee settlements. Sequoyah became a tribal hero, and, as one missionary observed, "the whole [eastern Cherokee] nation became an academy for the study of the [writing] system."

After staying in the East long enough to teach his syllabary to others, who could then teach it themselves, Sequoyah returned to Arkansas. Although he resumed his work as an artisan, he continued to teach his syllabary to anyone who was interested in learning how to use it. Soon the Cherokees in Arkansas were able to communicate in writing with those in the southern Appalachian country. Albert Gallatin, the pioneer American anthropologist, was among those astounded by the rapidity with which old and young Cherokees could master the syllabary of Sequoyah.

The introduction of Sequoyah's writing system had a tremendous impact on tribal society in the eastern Cherokee Nation. The vogue of writing in Cherokee swept like wildfire through the tribal domain, and soon American travelers in Cherokee country noticed directions for different paths inscribed on trees in Sequoyah's characters. Christian missionaries, who had labored in vain for years trying to transcribe the Cherokee language into written form, now hurried to translate the New Testament and other religious writings into the characters designed by Sequoyah. Not only was the syllabary officially adopted by the tribe, but also, on February 21, 1828, a bilingual tribal newspaper, the *Cherokee Phoenix,* made its appearance. For the first time in the history of the Indians of North America, the council proceedings and laws of a tribe were published in the native language. Sequoyah's invention was one of several factors that contributed to the formulation, diffusion, and perpetuation of a Cherokee tribal consciousness which solidified Cherokee national sentiment by the late 1820s. Sam Houston, who had lived for a time with the Cherokees in Arkansas afer resigning the governorship of Tennessee in 1829, once told Sequoyah that his invention was "worth more than a double handful of gold" to each Cherokee Indian.

In recognition of the remarkable achievement that Sequoyah had made to the Cherokee people, the tribal council in 1824 voted to award him a large silver medal. The medal was wrought in Washington under the supervision of John Ross, president of the upper house of the tribal council. On one side appeared a bust of Sequoyah with an inscription in English, "presented to George Gist by the General Council of the Cherokee Nation, for his ingenuity in The Invention of the Cherokee Alphabet, 1825." On the reverse side was an illustration of two pipes with crossed stems (possibly signifying the eastern and western Cherokees), encircled by the same inscription in Cherokee characters. Eastern tribal leaders hoped to honor Sequoyah by presenting the medal to him before a full council assembly, but the inventor preferred to remain in Arkansas. The medal was eventually forwarded to Sequoyah on January 12, 1832, with a congratulatory letter from John Ross, then the principal tribal chief. Sequoyah wore the medal with pride, but it apparently was not the one he was wearing when his portrait was painted in Washington in 1828.

Sequoyah journeyed to the white man's capital city in 1828

with a delegation of Cherokee leaders from Arkansas in order to seek redress for several grievances. Among these concerns were difficulties with fierce western tribes. The United States had granted the Cherokees land that included the historic hunting grounds of the Osage and Quapaw Indians. Other problems included boundary disputes with white settlers and the irregularity of annuity payments promised by the United States. Although Sequoyah and his fellow delegates had no authority to negotiate a cession or exchange of land, American officials on May 6, 1828, persuaded the delegation to sign a treaty ceding their land in Arkansas in exchange for a tract in present-day Oklahoma. Four members of the delegation, including Sequoyah, signed the document in Cherokee characters.

While in Washington, Sequoyah posed for artist Charles Bird King and, through an interpreter, was interviewed by American journalists. He also met various American dignitaries and representatives from other Indian tribes who were visiting the city. Interest in the Cherokee inventor was increased by the appearance of the first issue of the *Cherokee Phoenix*.

Like other members of his delegation, Sequoyah was apprehensive about the manner in which the people back home would react to news of the new treaty. Sequoyah himself was a direct beneficiary of certain provisions of the agreement. The United States had promised him $500 "for the great benefits he has conferred upon the Cherokee people, in the beneficial results which they are now experiencing from the use of the Alphabet discovered by him." Sequoyah also received assurances that he could locate and occupy a valuable saline in the new Cherokee country in exchange for the one he would have to abandon in Arkansas.

The delegation received an angry reception on its return to Arkansas. Many western Cherokees were fearful that much of the land they were to resettle on in present-day Oklahoma was of less value than the land they would have to leave behind. Sequoyah, however, quickly pointed out that the treaty promised many benefits, including permanent boundaries, reimbursement for improvements in Arkansas plus a cash settlement of $50,000, an educational annuity of $2,000 for ten years, and $1,000 for the purchase of a printing press with Cherokee characters. The Cherokees in Arkansas soon reconciled themselves to the bargain.

Sequoyah joined his Cherokee neighbors in moving from Arkansas to the wilderness on the eastern edge of Oklahoma. He selected a homesite and built a cabin near the saline the government had promised him. The saline was located in today's Sequoyah County 12 miles northeast of the present-day town of Sallisaw. Thanks to the saline and to the fertile acreage at his disposal, he soon prospered. He continued teaching his syllabary to people in neighboring towns and to visitors, and he also tutored students in a special school established by leaders of the resettled band.

During the years following Sequoyah's move to the new Cherokee country in Oklahoma, American travelers eagerly sought an interview with the inventor of the Cherokee syllabary. His home was near the military road running from Fort Smith in Arkansas to Fort Gibson just across the Oklahoma-Arkansas line. Army officers and other travelers to the West had little trouble making their way there for a visit. One such caller was Captain John Stuart of the U.S. Seventh Infantry who, according to the *Arkansas Gazette,* described his host in this manner:

> George Guess, the inventor of the Cherokee alphabet, is a man of about sixty years of age. He is of middle stature, and of rather a slender form, and is slightly lame in one leg, from disease when young. His features are remarkably regular, and his face well formed, and rather handsome. His eyes are animated and piercing, showing indications of a brilliancy of intellect far superior to the ordinary portion of his fellow men. His manner is agreeable, and his deportment gentlemanly. He possesses a mild disposition, and is patient, but is energetic and extremely persevering and determined in the pursuit or accomplishment of any object on which he may fix his mind. He is inquisitive, and appears to be exceedingly desirous of acquiring information on all subjects. His mind seems to soar high and wide; and if he could have had the advantages of an enlightened education, he would no doubt have brought himself to rank high among the acknowledged great men of the age in which he lives. He has been in the habit, ever since he could apply his language in that way, of keeping a journal of all the passing events which he considered worthy of record: and has, at this time (it is said), quite a volume of such matter.

Another soldier who visited Sequoyah reported, "he has an extremely interesting, intelligent countenance, full of cheerful animation with an evident vein of good humor . . . [and he] habitually wears a shawl turban and dresses rudely, as if not caring for the outward man."

Sequoyah was a frequent visitor to nearby Dwight Mission, a station of the American Board of Commissioners for Foreign Missions. He especially enjoyed the intellectual atmosphere there, but he never became a Christian nor learned to speak, read, or write the English language. At the mission he was able to obtain copies of the *Cherokee Phoenix*. He took great pride in reading the columns of this bilingual newspaper printed in characters of his own invention. In 1835 the Christian missionary Samuel A. Worcester established a printing press in the western Cherokee country, and soon thousands of pages with Sequoyah's characters printed on them were available to the western Cherokees.

Events in the West were of special concern to the Cherokees in the East. Andrew Jackson may have been a hero to white people in Tennessee and elsewhere in the United States, but to the eastern Cherokees he was the spokesman for those seeking to expel them from their ever-diminishing domain. During the administrations of Jackson and his hand-picked successor, Martin Van Buren, these Cherokees came under unrelenting pressure to sign a treaty of removal. The resulting chaos led to the emergence of two rival Cherokee factions: the majority National party, led by the Chief John Ross, and the minority Treaty party, led by Major Ridge, his son John Ridge, and his nephew Elias Boudinot. When the Treaty party signed what National party leaders called a "fraudulent treaty" in 1835, the fate of the eastern Cherokee Nation was sealed. By late March of 1839, all but a handful of Cherokees who hid out in the Great Smoky Mountains had completed a forced exodus to the West along the *Nunna-da-ult-sun-yi* ("the trail where they cried"). About 4,000 of these people—men, women and children—died as a result of the hardships of the trip or the circumstances surrounding their capture and detention before emigration.

On June 22, 1839, just three months after the last contingent of eastern Cherokees arrived in the West, Major Ridge, John Ridge, and Elias Boudinot—the leaders of the Treaty party—were brutally assassinated. A virtual intratribal war erupted over the question of which faction—western Cherokees or Old Settlers, the National party, or the Treaty party—would supply the leadership to govern the "reunited" tribe. Sequoyah, an Old Settler, became one of the leading spokesmen for moderation. He labored arduously to have all differences between the various factions settled, to use his words, "amicably and satisfactorily."

Under the influence of Sequoyah and other moderates, an Act of Union was adopted on July 12, 1839, and "one body politic" designated "the Cherokee Nation" was declared to be in existence. At a meeting at Tahlequah, the new Cherokee capital, John Ross unanimously was elected principal chief, and Joseph Vann, an Old Settler, was elected second principal chief. The other leading officers were all Old Settlers. In 1841 the supposedly reunited Cherokee Nation bestowed on Sequoyah an annual income for life. This was possibly the first literary pension in American history. Sequoyah was obviously pleased, but also was fearful for the future of his people. Tribal unity was not a reality because fundamental differences remained between various factions.

In the months following the adoption of the Act of Union, Sequoyah dreamed of reuniting *all* Cherokees and of finding enough similarities among various Indian languages to permit him to devise a system of writing for all Indian peoples. Concerned about news of atrocities being committed by Texans against Cherokees, he persuaded a battered remnant of a band of Cherokees that had settled in Texas years earlier to rejoin the main body of the Cherokee Nation. Then, in the summer of 1842, Sequoyah left Oklahoma with his eldest son Tessee and a small party of Cherokee horsemen pledged to secrecy. Their purpose was to locate a band of Cherokees that supposedly had settled somewhere in the Southwest years before. In August of 1843, while still engaged in his quest, the elderly Sequoyah succumbed, possibly from dysentary, near San Fernando, Tamaulipas, Mexico. According to legend, he was wearing the medal awarded him by the Cherokee tribal council when he was buried in a still-undiscovered grave. His journal, to the chagrin of future generations of Cherokee and white historians, apparently was buried with him.

Sequoyah's important contribution to his people has led some writers to hail him as "the finest intelligence of the American Indians." He has been acclaimed a genius by whites and Indians alike. Today the log cabin that Sequoyah built in Oklahoma stands as a shrine. Many honors, including the naming of the giant redwood trees of California after him, have been bestowed upon Sequoyah. Crippled in body but strong in mind and spirit, Sequoyah stood tall like a giant redwood tree. Although Sequoyah served the Cherokee Nation both as a warrior and a peacemaker, he is best remembered as the Cadmus of his people. Like Cadmus, the Phoenician prince of classical mythology, he introduced writing to his people and planted seeds which still bear fruit today. Few individuals in the long history of the world have made such a remarkable contribution to the development of their people as Sequoyah, the Cherokee Cadmus.

SUGGESTED READINGS

It is ironic that Sequoyah, who often is referred to as "the greatest of all Cherokees," has not been the subject of recent scholarly attention. Although more than a dozen biographical sketches have been written about him, there still are many significant unanswered questions about his life. Sequoyah's career still awaits a comprehensive biography. Among the most often cited studies are George M. Foster, *Se-Quo-Yah, The American Cadmus and Modern Moses* (Philadelphia, 1885); Grant Foreman, *Sequoyah* (Norman, 1938); and Jack Frederick Kilpatrick, *Sequoyah of Earth & Intellect* (Austin, 1965).

Traveller Bird, *Tell Them They Lie: The Sequoyah Myth* (Los Angeles, 1971) is a controversial revisionist account by a descendant of Sequoyah which should be read in conjunction with Raymond D. Fogelson, "On the Varieties of Indian History: Sequoyah and Traveller Bird," *Journal of Ethnic Studies, II* (Spring 1974), 105-112, and John White, Review of *Tell Them They Lie:* Elaborate Fabrication," *Indian Historian,* V (Spring 1972), 45-46.

Articles relating to specific aspects of Sequoyah's life include a study of "The Life and Work of Sequoyah," by John B. Davis, *Chronicles of Oklahoma,* VIII (June 1930), 149-180; Albert V. Goodpasture, "The Paternity of Sequoyah, the Inventor of the Cherokee Alphabet," *Chronicles of Oklahoma,* I (October 1921), 121-125; Samuel C. Williams, "Nathaniel

Gist, Father of Sequoyah," *East Tennessee Historical Society Publications,* V (January 1933), 39-54; and Grant Foreman, "The Story of Sequoyah's Last Days," *Chronicles of Oklahoma,* II (March 1934), 25-41.

General histories of the Cherokees which offer insights regarding Sequoyah's life include James Mooney, *Historical Sketch of the Cherokee* (1900, reprinted, Chicago, 1975); Marion L. Starkey, *The Cherokee Nation* (New York, 1946); Henry Thompson Malone, *Cherokees of the Old South: A People in Transition* (Athens, 1956); and Grace Steele Woodward, *The Cherokees* (Norman, 1963). For information on the Cherokees in Tennessee, see Ronald N. Satz, *Tennessee's Indian Peoples: From White Contact to Removal, 1540-1840* (Knoxville), 1979). An important bibliographic source for the serious student of Cherokee history is Rennard Strickland, "In Search of Cherokee History," a bibliographical foreword to the second printing of Morris L. Wardell, *A Political History of The Cherokee Nation 1838-1907* (1938, reprinted, Norman, 1977).

DAVID CROCKETT
by J. Ralph Randolph

> *Be always sure you're right–THEN GO AHEAD!*
> *Motto of Crockett*

David Crockett the man and Davy Crockett the legend are almost impossibly intertwined in the minds of Tennesseans and other Americans. Crockett was frontiersman, Indian fighter, bear hunter, state legislator, and United States congressman. He was unusual in American politics in that he was alternately praised for his backwoods humor and wit and condemned as an ignorant, barely literate boor by both major political parties of his day. Few if any of his contemporaries questioned his honesty, but many considered him almost unbelievably naive even after more than a decade in politics.

David Crockett was born August 17, 1786, "at the mouth of Lime Stone, on the nola-Chucky River" in Greene County, Tennessee. This fact and most of what is known of Crockett's first 20 years appeared in *A Narrative of the Life of David Crockett,* for which Crockett supplied most of the information. His ancestors almost certainly were Scotch-Irish, part of that great migration which contributed so much to our nation's expansion. John, his father, and his grandfather, for whom he was named, along with other members of the family were among the first settlers in the territory. When the Crocketts came to eastern Tennessee, not all of the Indians had accepted white settlement. In the spring of 1777 the grandparents of David Crockett were killed by raiding Indians.

John Crockett was a sometimes farmer, miller, and tavern keeper. He seems to have moved frequently during his life— unsuccessfully seeking to escape poverty. When David was seven or eight years old, a mill built by his father and a partner was destroyed by "Noah's fresh," and the family moved to Jefferson County. There John Crockett opened a small tavern on the road between Abbington, Virginia, and Knoxville. He later followed his son's moves across the state and died near David's home in West Tennessee.

When he was 12 years old, David was hired out to help drive some cattle to Rockbridge County, Virginia (for much of the next eight years he worked to help his father pay debts). Arriving at their destination, his employer persuaded the youngster to remain with him, perhaps because David at first believed some arrangement to that effect had been made with his father. However, a few weeks later David met some wagoners who often stopped at his father's tavern. According to the *Narrative,* The 12-year-old slipped away during the night and in two hours walked seven miles in snow sometimes waist high to joint he wagoners. After more adventures, David returned home.

When David was 13 his father decided he needed to go to school. This attempt at education was short-lived. David had a fight with "a boy much large and older." Because he feared the schoolmaster "would lick me up, as bad as I had the boy," he stopped going to classes. With the help of his brothers, he hid the fact from his father for some time. When his truancy at last was discovered, David was ordered to school, but refused and instead ran away from home. For the next two and a half years, he traveled, usually in Virginia, but on one occasion he went as far north as Baltimore. During this time he often earned his keep and sometimes a little more by working for wagoners. He also indicated that he worked for a hatter for 18 months. When he returned home is not certain, but it probably was in the spring of 1802.

David spent the next year repaying his father's debts to two men. He genuinely liked the second man, "an honest old Quaker, by the name of John Kennedy." After he had repaid the debt, he continued working for the men for some money of his own, and fell "head over heels in love" with a niece of the Quaker who came to visit. However, he soon discovered that she was engaged and began to court another young lady. He related that he "continued paying my respects to her, until I got to love her as bad as I did the Quaker's

David Crockett. *Photograph courtesy the State Library and Archives.*

niece; and I would have agreed to fight a whole regiment of wild cats if she would only have said she would have me." Unfortunately for him, after he had secured a marriage license in October 1805, the object of his desires married another. This unexpected development caused him to write that "my heart was bruised, and my spirits were broken down; so I bid her farewell, and turned my lonesome and miserable steps back homeward, concluding that I was only born for hardship, misery and disappointment."

His spirits soon mended and within a year he had met, wooed, and married Polly Finley. Polly's mother seems to have wanted her daughter to marry someone else, despite David's "salting the cow to catch the calf." However, the young couple and Polly's father overcame the objections, and David and Polly were married in August 1806. They had three children: John Wesley, born in 1807; William, born in 1809; and later a daughter, Margaret, who was called Polly.

With a gift of "two likely cows and calves" from the forgiving Mr. Finley and 15 dollars worth of merchandise from the Quaker friend, the Crocketts began farming on rented property. With a growing family and "paying high rent" Crockett decided to move. He indicated that the family went to Lincoln County in 1809, but court records indicated that the move came in the early autumn of 1811. Less than two years later the family moved to Franklin County, about 10 miles north of Winchester and a few miles north of the present state line.

During the summer of 1813 a war between the whites and a portion of the Creek nation, the Red Sticks, began. In addition to the Indians' hatred of the settlers' gradual and consistent encroachment onto Indian lands, the British, with the blessings of Spaniards in Florida, were supplying the Creeks with weapons and encouraging the war. During that summer some 180 whites ambushed a smaller force of Indians in northern Alabama. At noon on August 30, 1893, the Creeks retaliated at Fort Mims. The fort contained 265 soldiers and nearly 200 civilians when the Indians poured through the open gate of the fort, which had not been properly prepared for an attack. In what Crockett called "a most bloody butchery," about 500 men, women, and children were killed.

In September that year, Crockett, whose "dander was up," and many of his neighbors joined the Tennessee Volunteer Mounted Riflemen commanded by their elected captain, Francis Jones. Leaving his tearful wife and children in their newly established home, Private Crockett and the militia marched into Alabama.

The career of Crockett in the Creek War was honorable—but not distinguished. He did not take part in the Battle of Horseshoe Bend, which ended the war, nor did he have the opportunity to serve with General Jackson at the Battle of New Orleans. The most important engagement during his first enlistment was at Tallusahatchee, a Creek town near present-day Gadsden. Nearly 200 Creeks were killed, about 80 were captured, and several hundred escaped in the brief but bloody fight. The account of the battle in the *Narratives* leaves no doubt that Crockett possessed the typical frontier attitude toward Indians. In a manner completely lacking in sympathy, he told of women and children being killed. General Jackson reported to Governor Blount, "We have retaliated for the destruction of Fort Mims."

After a spring and summer of farming, Crockett reenlisted for six months in September 1814 as a 3rd Sergeant. The army's objective was Pensacola, which many Americans saw as the source of their problems with the Indians and the British. After their defeat at Horseshoe Bend, many Creeks had fled to the Spanish town and were being used by the British as a threat to Mobile and New Orleans. Crockett and his group of militia missed the capture of Pensacola, and when Jackson and the main portion of the army marched to New Orleans and fame, Crockett's regiment was assigned to protect the army's rear from the Creeks, who had fled to the nearby swamps.

In the *Narrative* Crockett seems to have deliberately fostered an error concerning his activities during the Creek war. He related that he was among the "mutineers" who wanted to leave and go home. The men were ill-equipped and often near starvation, and they wanted food, more suitable clothing, and "fresh horses" before another campaign. Besides, Crockett stated "our sixty days had long been out, and that was the time we entered for." In reality, Crockett's first enlistment was for 90 days, and when the incident occurred he was on leave to go home and get horses.

The reason for the misrepresentation seems to have been that, when the *Narrative* was written in the 1830s, Crockett was a political foe of Jackson, and he evidently wanted to show a long-standing ability to clash with "Old Hickory." In any case, the "mutiny" of the volunteers was put down by Jackson and the regular army troops, and the general then used the volunteers to put down unrest among the regulars.

The two years which followed his discharge from the militia in 1815 were not good ones for Crockett. That summer his wife died, leaving him with three young children. In 1816 he solved this problem by marrying Elizabeth Patton, a widow of one of his neighbors who had died in the Creek War. She had two children, George and Margaret Ann. Crockett and his second wife had four children. Despite Elizabeth having "a snug little farm," Crockett was dissatisfied and sought new land. He and three companions explored land in Alabama which had been opened by the Creek War. During his return trip he became severely ill, probably with malaria. When he finally reached his home, he found that he had been reported dead. He had become separated from his companions, and they had met some men who supposedly had seen Crockett die and helped bury him. The "revived" explorer stated, "I know'd this was a whopper of a lie, as soon as I heard it." Sometime in 1817 the Crocketts moved to Shoal Creek near the center of Lawrence County.

In Lawrence County, Crockett began his public career, one which eventually was to bring him national fame and bitter disappointment. First appointed informally by his neighbors as a justice of the peace, he soon was confirmed in the position by the state legislature. He stated that at this time he was nearly illiterate, perhaps an exaggeration, but his honesty and sense of justice made him popular. He next was asked by a "Capt. Matthews" to be a candidate for the position of First Major of the county militia. Crockett had been elected a lieutenant of the Franklin County militia, and he agreed. But he discovered that the captain, who was a candidate for the position of colonel of militia, was actually supporting his own son for major. Crockett changed his mind, ran for colonel, and won.

In February of 1821, Colonel Crockett, as he was to be greeted for the rest of his life, became a candidate for the state legislature from Lawrence and Hickman counties. He stated that he knew little of state or even local politics or problems, but he was respected for his honesty, could entertain an audience with his backwoods humor, and had a quick wit. At one large gathering of voters he was called upon to speak before his opponent. After telling a few lively stories, he stated, "I took care to remark that I was as dry as a powder horn, and I thought it was time for us all to wet our whistles a little; and so I put off to the liquor stand, and was followed by the greater part of the crowd." His opponent was left with "mighty few." Crockett easily won the election.

Changes in the American political scene also helped David Crockett in this campaign and in his others. He was in many ways representative of his constituents. Like many of them, he had little education, he had little wealth, and he had proven his devotion to his state and nation in war. In the genteel politics of Washington and Jefferson, Crockett would have little chance to hold office, but by the 1820s the "common man" was seeking and gaining political power.

Crockett's service in the 14th General Assembly reveals the beginning of his efforts to help the settlers of West Tennessee, especially the poor "squatters." He voted for a bill that would better regulate surveying in that area, and for another calling for a constitutional convention which was needed to correct the underrepresentation of that rapidly growing portion of the state, as well as to correct inequitable land taxes. During this assembly Crockett gained the title of "the gentleman from canes." The term was used insultingly to refer to Crockett by another member, but the frontiersman successfully poked fun at his adversary's dress to the delight of the other members. Thereafter Crockett was amicably referred to by that title.

During the legislative sessions, disaster struck at home. His grist and powder mill and his "large distillery" were destroyed in a flood. He agreed with his wife that his creditors should get everything that remained, and the Crocketts made plans to move further west and begin once more.

Following the close of the assembly, Crockett, his son John Wesley, and another young man left to explore northwest Tennessee. Crockett selected a site on the Obion River in what was then

Carroll County for his new home. He liked the fact that "all sorts of game and wild vermints, except Buffalo" were plentiful. Of special delight to the hunter was the abundance of bears. This area was a part of the "Western District" which Jackson and James Shelby had purchased from the Chickasaw Indians only a few years previously. Their nearest neighbor was seven miles away.

Preparations were made for the family to move. A small cabin was built and a crop was planted before Crockett left for home. He attended a called session of the legislature, and by September of 1822 he had moved his family and "what little plunder I had." Next year he again was a candidate for the legislature. He indicated that he was put forth without his knowledge and as a joke. However, he waged a vigorous campaign, whereupon two of his opponents left the race in order to support a third, Dr. William E. Butler. Butler, who was related by marriage to Jackson, lost the campaign. A major issue apparently was Crockett's charge that Butler was an "aristocrat" because he had a rug, not bearskins, on his living room floor.

Crockett's legislative career was the occasion of his first break with the Jackson political forces of the state. The term of U.S. Senator John Williams had ended, and he desired reelection. Jackson wanted Williams' defeat and finally became a candidate himself. When the Tennessee legislature, which then elected senators, voted, Crockett cast his ballot with the minority for the incumbent. The western legislator indicated that he "thought the colonel [Williams] had honestly discharged his duty, and even the mighty name of Jackson wouldn't make me vote against him." Crockett continued to favor a constitutional convention and opposed a bill to use prison labor because many prisoners were debtors. He introduced a bill to free honest debtors from prison. During a second session of that General Assembly, approval was finally gained for a constitutional convention. The need for increased representation from the Western District was apparent in the fact Crockett by then was representing ten counties.

In 1825 Crockett ran for the congress against Colonel Wilson Alexander, the incumbent. Alexander's support of the Tariff of 1824 was unpopular in the district, but the local cotton prices were extremely good that year, $25 a hundred, and Alexander won by convincing the voters that the tariff was the cause.

The former legislator spent the next two years farming, hunting, and trying his hand at new ways to make money. He had two
boats built on Obion Lake and loaded them with pipe and barrel
staves. Meanwhile, the Tennessean was bear hunting with his eight
dogs, which he said were "as fierce as painters [panthers]." He
stated that before the winter ended, he had killed 105 bears which
kept him and his neighbors in meat. After beginning their voyage,
Crockett and his crew realized that they knew neither how to steer
the boats nor land them. A short distance above Memphis the boats
capsized, and Crockett nearly drowned. Rescued and taken to
Memphis, the party was given clothes and money by a friend of
Crockett, Marcus B. Winchester. During the 1827 congressional
campaign Crockett had a "good friend" who financed his efforts
and the evidence points to Winchester as that friend.

In 1827 Crockett ran for congress against Alexander. A third
candidate was General William Arnold, a prominent citizen of
Jackson and the area. The congressional district was large, and
Crockett campaigned vigorously. A severe decline in the price of
cotton hurt Alexander, and he and Arnold attacked each other
while ignoring the backwoodsman. The result was that Crockett
won by a sizeable margin.

When the new congressman reached Washington, he still considered himself a supporter of Jackson. He believed that "Old
Hickory" had been cheated out of the presidency in 1824 by a bargain of some kind between John Quincy Adams and Henry Clay.
However, Crockett quickly discovered that his concerns for West
Tennessee were not shared by James K. Polk, Jackson's spokesman in the House of Representatives, and other members from
the state.

Only a few days after entering congress, Crockett began work
on the Tennessee Vacant Land Bill, an endeavor which became an
obsession with him. The bill provided that all federal land which
was "vacant" in the legal sense, although it might be occupied by
"squatters," would be given to the state for educational purposes.
Representatives from West Tennessee wanted the land free or sold
as cheaply as possible, but not everyone agreed. The state government, with Polk as its spokesman, wanted the land surveyed and
sold to the highest bidder. Both sides could and did present strong

arguments. Polk and his supporters cited the need for funds to build colleges in the state. Crockett maintained that his constituents seldom saw the inside of any school, much less a college. Polk believed public money could be saved if the state surveyed the land and sold it through state land offices, which were already established. Crockett wanted the federal government to handle the transactions, believing that it would cost the settlers less. The frontiersman concluded that land speculator interests controlled the state and its spokesmen in congress. In one speech he thundered that "the rich require but little legislation. We should, at least occasionally, legislate for the poor."

Action on the bill was delayed in that congress and during the next one. Polk proposed a compromise of selling the land at 12½¢ an acre. Crockett at first believed that price was too high and opposed the amendment, but later voted for it. However, he was too late. The Jacksonians had grown tired of this thorn and would do nothing to help Crockett—and anything to hurt him with the voters of his district.

Doubtless the Tennessee land question was the cause of Crockett's break with Jackson and his party. However, Crockett and the Jacksonians differed over other matters. The question of the national government's involvement and responsibilities for improving roads and navigation of rivers and the removal of the Southeastern Indians also were important issues over which they disagreed. Crockett was the only Tennessean to vote against the Indian Removal Bill, opposition which is hard to explain. His grandparents had been killed by Indians, and he had grown up in an area where hatred of them was nearly unanimous. Furthermore, the Narrative, which was published three years after this vote, revealed no sympathy for native Americans. By the time the vote on the Indian bill was taken, Crockett simply apparently could not vote for any measure proposed by President Jackson.

Despite his failure to secure passage of the Tennessee land bill, his efforts were popular with the voters of his district. He easily won reelection in 1829. Meanwhile, his differences with Jackson had gained the attention of the Whigs, as the opposition party was coming to be called. Crockett's unusual and colorful character only added to his appeal. His appearance was not exceptional and his clothes were normal for gentlemen of the day, but his speech and mannerisms were considreed eccentric by Easterners. He began to have help in writing his speeches, probably by Whig newspaper editors. Whig members of Congress also realized that support of his proposals caused embarrassment for Jackson and his party.

The Jacksonians got their first revenge in the election of 1831. The campaign was the first where Crockett was in open opposition to Jackson. The incumbent's opponent was William Fitzgerald, a lawyer from Dresden, Tennessee. Crockett stated that he "was hunted down like a wild varment" by the Jacksonian newspapers and "every little pinhook lawyer." He was charged with wasting $560 of taxpayers' money for missing votes in Congress (at $8 a vote). But Crockett believed trickery really caused his defeat. Announcements were made without his knowledge that he would appear at a certain place to explain his opposition to Jackson. "Small-fry lawyers" would then appear and harangue the crowd to defeat him. He lost by some 500 votes out of more than 16,000 cast.

Crockett again ran for Congress in 1833. *The Life and Adventures of Colonel David Crockett of West Tennessee,* published early that year in Cincinnati, was an effort to help his reelection chances. Much of the material in the work came from Crockett, but it also was filled with tall tales and outlandish stories. It seemed to hurt him more than help, and in the *Narrative* of a year later he disavowed knowledge of the author. Despite the *Life and Adventures,* Crockett won a very close election over Fitzgerald. The Jacksonian was a poor speaker, and newspapers seemed more equitable in their coverage of the candidates.

Crockett's last session of congress saw him making an unsuccessful attempt to secure passage of the Tennessee land bill—and a more successful attempt by the Whigs to use the West Tennessean. His speeches, which were being written or "improved" for him, received extensive coverage in Whig newspapers. There was considerable discussion of him as a possible candidate for the presidency. The Whigs also decided to show him off to the urban masses.

Beginning in April of 1834, Crockett made a "towar" [tour] of the major cities on the eastern seaboard. In Baltimore, Philadelphia, New York City, and Boston huge crowds awaited his arrival in each city and at his appearances in theaters. He dined with local

Whig dignitaries and visited important sites. Unfortunately he did not seem to realize how carefully staged the crowds were nor the extent to which he was being used.

Adam Huntsman, a lawyer, was his opponent in the election of 1835. Huntsman was an able campaigner and popular in the district. Crockett lost the election, perhaps because the Jacksonian support of Huntsman was too great or perhaps because of his failure to secure the land bill. Whatever the causes of the defeat, Crockett was bitter. His increasing debts added to his problems, and he resolved to move to Texas. Less than a month after the voting, Crockett, his nephew William Patton, a brother-in-law, Abner Buyin, and a neighbor, Lindsey Tinkle, left Tennessee. In Memphis the group had a farewell party at the Union Hotel with some friends. Perhaps having drunk too much and still brooding over his defeat, Crockett announced that Tennesseans could "go to hell and I will go to Texas."

After crossing Arkansas, the party traveled up the Red River to Clarksville, Texas, and on to Nacogdoches. There Crockett and Patton took the oath of allegiance to the provisional government. The other two Tennesseans seem to have returned home about this time. Texas then was in revolt against Mexico and was about to be invaded by a large army under General Antonio López de Santa Anna. A small group of volunteers was assembling at San Antonio De Béxar to try to stop or at least to delay that force. Crockett and perhaps his nephew joined a small party hastening to the small Texas town. They arrived there in early February of 1836.

On February 23, Santa Anna demanded the surrender of the Alamo, the old mission being used as a fortress. The Texans refused, and a bombardment began on the night of the 24th. At dawn on Sunday, March 6, more than 2,000 Mexican troops stormed the Alamo defended by about 150 able-bodied men. Only Mrs. Susanna Dickinson, her daughter, and a few Negroes and Mexicans survived the slaughter. Crockett and the others died, but their gallant sacrifice gave Sam Houston and the Texas army time to prepare. Without the heroic stand at the Alamo, the movement for Texas' independence might have failed.

Historians and others have argued over the circumstances of David Crockett's death from the time of the fall of the Alamo. Regardless of the charges and counter-charges, Crockett, the heroic frontiersman, had died in the hearts of Americans. The legends of Davy Crockett began as early as the publication of the *Life and Adventure* in 1833. The *Narrative,* and especially the Crockett *Almanacs,* which began in 1835, added to the folklore. More recently, the popularity of the movies *The Alamo* and the Walt Disney movie and television series about Crockett indicates the continuing interest in Davy. Coonskin caps and the song, "King of the Wild Frontier," captured the imagination of children and adults alike. In 1948 Estes Kefauver campaigned with the coonskin cap symbol for the U.S. Senate. Serious scholars of American folklore have praised the importance of these legends and that these have helped shape modern America.

David Crockett should be remembered not only for what he did at the Alamo, but also for his efforts to help the people of Tennessee and as a symbol of courage and devotion for millions of Americans.

SUGGESTED READINGS

The single most important contemporary source for the study of Crockett is *A Narrative of the Life of David Crockett of the State of Tennessee* (Philadelphia, 1834). The information in it, which can be verified by other material, is generally accurate except as to dates and election returns. The *Narrative* was "ghostwritten" by Thomas Chilton based on information provided by the subject. The reprint edition published by the University of Tennessee Press (Knoxville, 1973), annotated by James A. Shackford and Stanley J. Folmsbee, is a valuable piece of scholarship.

The *Life and Adventures of Colonel David Crockett of West Tennessee* (Cincinnati, 1833) contains much of the same information as the *Narrative,* but also has numerous "tall tales" concerning the subject. Although Crockett later disavowed knowledge of the "ghostwriter," Matthew St. Clair Clarke, he knew him and must have furnished much of the information. Within a year after it was published, the *Life and Adventure* was reprinted with only a few changes as *Sketches and Eccentricities of Colonel David Crockett of West*

Tennessee (New York, 1833). *An Account of Col. Crockett's Tour in the North and Down East* (Philadelphia, 1835) was Whig propaganda based primarily on newspaper accounts of the trip.

Except for some information taken from two Crockett letters, the spurious *Col. Crockett's Exploits and Adventures in Texas* (Philadelphia, 1836) was the result of a publisher's exploitation of a hero, and is of little or no use in the study of the historic Crockett. Likewise the Crockett *Almanacs*, the first being published in Nashville in 1835 and then issued for years, were popular efforts to use the Tennessean's name. Crockett had no part in their production.

James A. Shackford, *David Crockett: The Man and the Legend*, ed. by John B. Shackford (Chapel Hill, 1956), is the standard Crockett biography and does much to separate the "man" from the "legend." It is completely sympathetic to its subject. Walter Blair, *Davy Crockett, Frontier Hero; the Truth as He Told It, The Legend as Friends Built It* (New York, 1955) and Constance M. Rourke, *Davy Crockett* (New York, 1934), are generally entertaining and valuable studies which emphasize the legendary Crockett. Dan Kilgore's *How Did Davy Die?* (College Station, 1978), is the latest study of that controversy. Based primarily on Mexican sources only recently available, it concludes that Crockett did not die in the midst of battle.

7

NATHAN BEDFORD FORREST
by William R. Majors

"Git thar fustest with the mostest" was the strategy applied by "that devil," Confederate General Nathan Bedford Forrest, for achieving his military objectives. No leader of the American Civil War, North or South, had a better record of accomplishing his immediate goals. Thus Forrest's place among the outstanding American military leaders cannot be challenged. Union General William T. Sherman acknowledged this when he declared that Forrest "was the most remarkable man our Civil War produced on either side . . . . He had a genius which was to me incomprehensible. . . ." Forrest has been called the "wizard of the saddle," the Confederacy's greatest cavalryman and Tennessee's greatest Confederate. Because he had little military experience and even less training prior to the Civil War, one writer has described Forrest as an "untutored military genius." Yet he became the South's most hated and feared general.

Although legend has depicted Forrest as violent and profane—a veritable maniac—he was normally mild and quiet in manner, at times even kindhearted and considerate in nature. However, in anger or in the excitement of battle, he could become a savage and courageous fighter without impairing his judgment. He often rode forth with his men to join in battle and possibly killed as many as 30 men. He was wounded three times, once by a subordinate who disagreed with an order, and it is said that 29 mounts were shot from under him in combat. Standing a ramrod straight six feet two inches in height and weighing a muscular 200 pounds, Forrest was an imposing figure with the bearing of a dynamic leader. Nevertheless he was generally regarded by those who did not know him as an illiterate, uncouth frontier ruffian. Although he had little formal education, except for poor spelling, he expressed himself easily and fluently. Certainly there was little in Forrest's humble origin to suggest that he would become the South's most magnificent field leader and a genuine native folk hero.

Nathan Bedford Forrest was born the son of William and Mariam Beck Forrest on July 13, 1821, in a small log cabin near Chapel Hill in what was then Bedford County, Tennessee. In 1836, the place of his birth became a part of the newly formed Marshall County. Little is known about the Forrest ancestry. Bedford's great-grandfather, Shadrach Forrest, who may have been born in England, lived for a time in western Virginia and moved to Orange County, North Carolina, sometime between 1730 and 1740. His grandfather, Nathan, who possibly served as a soldier in the American Revolution, was born in North Carolina and lived there most of his life. About 1806, Nathan, accompanied by his aging father Shadrach and his family, which included his young son, William, migrated to Sumner County, Tennessee, and settled near present-day Gallatin. Shadrach died shortly thereafter, and Nathan then moved to the Duck River valley in Bedford County where William grew to manhood and married Mariam Beck, whose family was among the early settlers in the area. William and Mariam Forrest's children included six boys, with Bedford the eldest, and three girls, one of whom was a twin born with Bedford. William was a blacksmith by trade and operated a small farm on the side. He apparently provided a modest livelihood for his family, but in 1834, for reasons not clear—perhaps it was frontier restlessness—William moved his large brood to the recently opened Indian territory in northern Mississippi and settled near Salem in Tippa County.

The Forrests were not well established in Mississippi when tragedy struck. William died in 1837, leaving his wife still carrying their last child and Bedford not yet 16 years of age. Mariam Forrest, a large woman, almost six feet in height and weighing nearly 180 pounds, was strong willed and perhaps a bit imperious. With a dominant personality, she demanded obedience from her children and easily earned their respect. Undoubtedly she could have raised her family without the assistance of a man, but custom required

Nathan Bedford Forrest. *From the author's collection.*

that the eldest son become, in effect, the head of the household. Bedford soon proved equal to the task, although it required long hours of hard labor in a struggle for survival in that wilderness environment. He also quickly demonstrated a willingness to assume an adult role when, after shooting an ox which had been feasting in the Forrest cornfield, Bedford confronted the angry owner and forced his hasty retreat.

Life was difficult in those years. It involved toiling from dawn to dusk clearing land or cultivating the crops and then working into the night by firelight making moccasins, leggins, and other articles of clothing for the children. There were no luxuries and no time for schooling—even if educational facilities had been available. Disease made life yet more difficult; two brothers and all three sisters, including Bedford's twin, Fanny, died from typhoid fever, and Bedford himself almost succumbed to the infection. But by hard work, good management, and some successful small-scale trading in horses and cattle, young Bedford achieved relative prosperity within four years, and the family was reasonably comfortable. He felt free, therefore, to leave the family in 1841 when he volunteered to join a company of soldiers being recruited at Holly Springs, Mississippi, to assist the Lone Star Republic of Texas in its fight to stay independent of Mexico. Mismanagement of funds led to the disbanding of the company in transit at New Orleans, but Bedford accompanied a remnant that proceeded on to Houston, Texas. Upon arrival, he discovered that no war was in progress and that his services were not needed. Without funds, he was forced to work at hard labor splitting rails in order to earn his way back to Mississippi. Bedford returned in 1842, a little older and wiser— and with few illusions about the glories of military adventures.

With his mother and brothers comfortable, Bedford Forrest turned to pursuits other than frontier farming. Soon after returning from Texas, he joined an uncle, Jonathan Forrest, in the mercantile business in Hernando, Mississippi, a community about 20 miles south of Memphis, Tennessee. North Mississippi had not lost its frontier character, and even the most sober citizens were sometimes forced into violent quarrels. In 1845, in an incident that was not uncommon to the area, Jonathan Forrest was killed in a quarrel with four men. Bedford then entered the fight, killed one of the assailants with a pistol, and, with only a Barlow knife for a weapon, routed the others without assistance. The mercantile establishment entirely in his hands, Bedford soon demonstrated business acumen, expanded into brick manufacturing, and organized and operated a stage line between Memphis and Hernando. Not all of his ventures were entirely successful, but he gradually accumulated capital and began buying land. He also became involved in matters of the heart. In 1845 he began courting Mary Ann Montgomery, a descendant of Revolutionary War hero General Richard Montgomery, who had been killed in the storming of Quebec in 1775. Although Bedford drank little, if any, and did not use tobacco in any form, Mary Ann's minister foster father at first refused to give his consent to marriage because he objected to Bedford's gambling habit and hearty use of profane language. But persistence paid off, and they were married in September of 1845. Mary Ann Forrest was quiet and refined in manner, and, although she had a better formal education, they were compatible and the marriage was apparently a happy one. Two children were born to the Forrests, a boy, William, or Willie as he was called, and a girl, Fanny, who died at the age of five. In 1851, Bedford Forrest moved his family to the booming river town of Memphis where he established a cotton, real estate, and slave trading brokerage and soon became a successful and respected businessman. Although he earned a reputation as a quiet, industrious, and sober citizen, Memphis was a rough river town and incidents of violence were common. In 1857, Bedford gained notoriety by single-handedly saving an accused murderer from a lynch mob estimated to be about 3,000, thus adding to his growing fame for boldness and courage. Indicative of his popularity in Memphis, Forrest was elected alderman in 1858 and reelected in 1859. Meanwhile, he had acquired two plantations in Mississippi, one in Coahoma County and the other in Tunica County. Early in 1859 he gave up his brokerage, resigned as alderman, and moved to Mississippi to manage his estates. For some reason he returned to Memphis later that same year and was immediately elected to serve out his own unexpired term as alderman. By the onset of the Civil War, Nathan Bedford Forrest was far removed from his plebeian origins; he was, in 1861, a wealthy slave-holding cotton planter worth an estimated $1,500,000.

Forrest's political philosophy was simple and practical, and he had no illusions about the issues facing the South in 1861. He believed that slavery was the central problem and that the policies of the Republican party, which had gained control of the national government in 1861, were a threat to that institution and to the Southern way of life. He was willing, if not eager, to fight to defend the static feudal society of the South and the dominance of the planter aristocracy—of which he was now a member. On June 14, 1861, he enlisted in the Confederate cause as a private in the 7th Tennessee Cavalry, along with his 14-year-old son, Willie, and his youngest brother Jeffrey. Except for John, who was disabled because of wounds suffered during the Mexican War, Bedford's other brothers were just as quick to volunteer, and all served with distinction. But the Civil War took a heavy toll. Aaron died of pneumonia in the winter of 1864; Jessie was disabled by wounds suffered in battle; Bill also suffered a non-disabling combat wound; and Jeffrey was killed in an engagement at Okolona, Mississippi, just prior to receiving his promotion to brigadier general. Mariam Forrest, Bedford's mother, had re-married, and all three sons by her second husband also served in the Confederate army.

Because of his reputation as both an outstanding citizen in his community and as a bold and courageous fighter, Bedford Forrest was given a commission as lieutenant colonel by Tennessee Governor Isham G. Harris, who authorized him to recruit, arm, and equip a battalion of rangers. He went about his task with dispatch and soon recruited eight companies and 650 troopers who were mustered into the Confederate army in October of 1861; however, he had to use his own funds to arm his command. Forrest quickly demonstrated his audacity by procuring guns from Louisville, Kentucky, despite the presence of active Union sympathizers in that area.

Forrest's battalion was initially assigned to the western sector's defense line which stretched from Columbus, Kentucky, on the Mississippi River, through Bowling Green, Kentucky, in the center to Cumberland Gap in the east. His first combat engagement took place at Sacramento, Kentucky, where he routed a Union scouting party, and his unit immediately earned a reputation for ferocious fighting. When the Union army under General Ulysses S. Grant began an offensive in the west, Forrest was directed to assist General John B. Floyd in the defense of Fort Donelson on the Cumberland River near the Kentucky-Tennessee border. Demonstrating a lack of resolution after the fort was surrounded and sieged, Floyd decided to surrender. Protesting, Forrest took his unit and cut through the enemy lines to safety and withdrew to Nashville, Tennessee. Believing that he could not hold Nashville in the face of the Union offensive, the Confederate commander in the west, General Albert S. Johnston, ordered the evacuation of that city and the establishing of a line of defense further south. Forrest was promoted to full colonel and ordered to Huntsville, Alabama, for rest and rehabilitation. By that time, with the addition of new recruits, his command was a full regiment.

Following the evacuation of Nashville, the Army of Tennessee, as the Confederate forces in the west were called, took up a defense line that stretched the length of Tennessee but was anchored at Corinth, Mississippi, where the Mobile and Ohio railroad junctioned with the Memphis to Charleston line. Because the latter railroad was an important link connecting both Charleston, South Carolina, and Richmond, Virginia, with the west, the Confederates considered it vital to keep that line of communication open. Grant began moving up the Tennessee River and in mid-March of 1862 landed a large army at Pittsburg Landing, a few miles north of Corinth just over the Tennessee line. Back at full strength, Forrest's command was ordered to join other units assembling in the Corinth area. His scouts reported that Union General Don Carlos Buell had begun moving his army from Nashville in the direction of Pittsburg Landing. General Johnston then decided to mass an attack on Grant's position at Shiloh Church before Buell could arrive, and Colonel Forrest's regiment, along with Colonel George Maney's 1st Tennessee Infantry, was assigned to protect the right flank.

The surprise assault began on Sunday, April 6, and despite a poorly organized and confusing operation, Union forces were steadily pushed back. By dark, the Confederates had seemingly carried the day, and the advance was halted. During the night, Forrest's scouts reported that heavy Union reinforcements were arriving, but his superiors seemed unconcerned. At dawn a massive

Union counterattack was hurled at the Confederate line with Forrest's regiment receiving the first blow. After a fierce struggle, General P. G. T. Beauregard, who had assumed command after General Johnston had been killed the previous day, directed the Confederate army to withdraw. The following day, the retreat was general, and Colonel Forrest was assigned the task of protecting the rear. To Forrest, the best defense was offense; in covering the retreating Confederate army, he so successfully ambushed, charged, and counterattacked the pressing Union forces under General W. T. Sherman that the Southern army escaped to Corinth. Forrest, however, in close combat, suffered a severe hip wound that necessitated several weeks of recuperation.

Shortly after returning to the regiment in northern Mississippi in June of 1862, Colonel Forrest was sent to Chattanooga to take command of a brigade of cavalry in the army led by General Braxton Bragg. He also was promoted to acting brigadier general and authorized to take offensive action. In mid-July of 1862, after careful preparation, Forrest led 1,000 men in a swift attack on the Union-held Murfreesboro. This effort resulted in the capture of more than 1,000 federal soldiers and valuable supplies. His success there, plus John Morgan's raids north of Nashville, encouraged Bragg to begin an ambitious invasion of Kentucky in late August with Louisville the primary objective. Bragg was ably assisted by Forrest, who guarded the left flank and continually harassed Union General Buell, who was moving his army from Nashville to protect Louisville. Forrest defeated a federal unit at Munfordville and began meticulously destroying bridges and the tracks of the Louisville and Nashville railroad. At that point Forrest was asked to give up his command to organize another brigade with headquarters at Murfreesboro. Permitted to take several companies that had served with him in Kentucky in 1861, Forrest established his command in October. Meanwhile, Bragg's invasion of Kentucky was brought to a halt at the battle of Perryville, and he was forced to withdraw to Tennessee.

Forrest assumed his new post and quickly recruited and organized a new brigade. Shortly thereafter, he was directed to make an expedition into West Tennessee to harass and and disrupt communications in that Union-occupied territory. Thus Forrest undertook his boldest operation yet, making the difficult crossing of the Tennessee River at Clifton on December 13-15, 1862. He defeated a Union garrison at Lexington in the first engagement of the campaign before advancing on Jackson. Although he made no attempt to capture Jackson, he laid waste to rail lines leading south of that city. Then he turned north and captured Trenton and Union City before retiring to the east. The federals attempted to prevent Forrest from reaching the Tennessee River but were repulsed in the battle of Parker's Crossroads. By January 3, 1863, the river had been re-crossed, thus ending a successful campaign. In just 15 days Forrest had kept the Union forces off balance while he wreaked havoc with transportation, killed or captured 2,500 men, and carried off 50 wagons and teams with an enormous amount of supplies. More than any previous engagement, the West Tennessee campaign of December, 1862, established Forrest's reputation as a daring and brilliant field commander.

Forrest's brigade returned to Columbia, Tennessee, just south of Nashville, for several weeks of rest. In February of 1863 he was directed to accompany Major General Joe Wheeler in an attempt to re-capture Fort Donelson. During the siege of that Fort, Forrest was ordered to make a frontal assault, and he made two unsuccessful charges before the attempt was abandoned. On returning to Tennessee, he was occupied with skirmishes in the area of Franklin and Brentwood until April when he was ordered to northern Alabama. Soon after arriving, Forrest's brigade was forced to defend the area against the Union's most ambitious cavalry raid of the war, led by Colonel Abel D. Straight. In a fierce five-day running battle across northern Alabama, Forrest finally forced the surrender of Straight's 1,500 men at Rome, Georgia. In May of 1863 General Forrest returned to Middle Tennessee for picket and scout duty and was involved in several small engagements. It was during this interval that a young lieutenant, Wills Gould, brooding over an unexplained transfer, shot Forrest. Despite a wound in the side, a furious Forrest seized Gould's pistol hand, opened a pen knife with his teeth, and then stabbed his assailant in the abdomen. Gould died a few days later but not before he and his general were reconciled.

In June of 1863 the Union army based at Nashville, commanded by General William Rosecrans, began a major offensive toward the southeast. Chattanooga, the gateway to Georgia and a rail link connecting Richmond in the east with the near southwest, was the objective. The Union army advanced steadily through the summer, and in September, General Bragg was forced to evacuate Chattanooga. Forrest received a minor wound in the fighting around that city but it was not sufficiently serious for him to leave his command. The armies of Rosecrans and Bragg faced off in a pitched battle at Chickamauga, just south of Chattanooga, in late September. In a bitter struggle the Confederate right wing, with Forrest in command of the extreme right, routed the Union army and forced its retreat to Chattanooga. Although Bragg had the federal army bottled up in that city, General Grant eventually was able to send in reinforcements and break the siege. Sharply critical of Bragg for what he considered a lack of initiative, Forrest submitted his resignation; however, Confederate President Jefferson Davis intervened and transferred Forrest to north Mississippi in November of 1863. The move in some respects was a reward, for he was given an independent command and was shortly promoted to major general.

Unfortunately, circumstances in Mississippi were not favorable. Upon his arrival at Okolona, Forrest discovered that his command was a poorly equipped force of only 271 men. Nevertheless, he resolved to make a recruiting expedition into West Tennessee, and on December 1, after receiving some reinforcements, headed his small army northward. After successfully breaching the Union lines near Grand Junction, Tennessee, he began recruiting, organizing guerrilla forces, and gathering supplies. Although West Tennessee was technically occupied by the Union, Forrest was able to move about the area in relative freedom because most of the federal forces were stationed along the Mississippi border from Memphis to the Tennessee River in the east. Union leaders became alarmed at his activities and tried to trap him, but Forrest eluded capture and returned to Mississippi late in December with 3,500 mounted men, 40 wagons and teams loaded with supplies, 200 head of beef, and 300 hogs. This was a remarkable expedition, for all other Confederate commands were having difficulty with recruitment and desertion.

In February of 1864 the Union army in the west launched an offensive aimed at invading Alabama and capturing Selma and Mobile. General William "Sooey" Smith marched southeast from Memphis to unite at Meridian, Mississippi, with General Sherman, who was to move a force east from Vicksburg, Mississippi. The expedition failed because Forrest so thoroughly disrupted Smith's march that he retired to Memphis before the month was over.

In the spring of 1864, General Forrest began his third invasion of West Tennessee. Moving north from Tupelo, Mississippi, he encountered little opposition and arrived at Jackson, Tennessee, on March 20. Three days later the federal garrison at Union City, Tennessee was defeated, and Forrest marched into Kentucky and seized Paducah on the 25th. As was his custom, Forrest accumulated as much as he could easily transport in the way of mounts, supplies, and equipment and carefully destroyed what he could not haul away. His main force then retired to the vicinity of Jackson; the most controversial event of Forrest's career took place shortly thereafter. About 40 miles north of Memphis on the Mississippi River stood the Union-held Fort Pillow, well fortified and garrisoned by about 550 men, of which approximately half were Negro. On April 12, in a surprise move, Forrest began an attack on the Fort and, when a demand for surrender was refused, stormed the garrison. More than half of the Union force at Fort Pillow was massacred, a majority of whom were Negro soldiers. The North was thoroughly aroused by the alleged atrocities, and congress subsequently conducted an investigation. What actually happened is not clear, but while the extent of the massacre was probably exaggerated, some indiscriminate killing of Negroes undoubtedly did take place. It is certain that Forrest did not order a slaughter, but he must have known that the presence of black soldiers had inflamed his men, and he apparently made no attempt to prevent unnecessary killing. Interestingly, he did not try to defend himself against the charges; but these claims only enhanced his reputation for savage fighting, and future foes were even less inclined to challenge him. His command remained in West Tennessee for two more weeks and engaged in several skirmishes before retiring to Mississippi.

Early in June, Union General Samuel Sturgis led a large expedition of cavalry and infantry from Memphis into Mississippi, and Forrest was ordered to repel him. Forrest fell upon Sturgis at Brice's Crossroads and thoroughly defeated the federal army, forcing its hasty retreat to Memphis. Another Union invasion of Mississippi, this time under the command of General A. J. Smith, marched out of Memphis in July. In a bloody battle in which Forrest received a painful wound in the foot, the Union army again was forced to retire to Memphis. In August, General Smith led still another invasion of Mississippi. To counter the offensive, Forrest selected 2,000 of his best troopers and, under cover of darkness, slipped in behind Smith and successfully raided Memphis on August 21. As a result of the attack, the third invasion of Mississippi was abandoned. Forrest turned to the east in September and raided Union outposts along the Tennessee River in northern Alabama and garrisons in adjacent portions of Middle Tennessee. The following month, he made a daring raid northward along the Tennessee River to Johnsonville and successfully destroyed a number of federal transports. Shortly thereafter he was ordered to join General John Bell Hood for a large-scale invasion of Middle Tennessee.

In the fall of 1864, with Union General W. T. Sherman pressing deep into Georgia, the Confederate leadership decided on an ambitious expedition to strike Nashville, an important point on Sherman's supply line. Hood's army, with Forrest in command of all cavalry, began its march on November 21. After losing opportunities to inflict severe defeat on Union forces, Hood finally reached Franklin, Tennessee, just south of Nashville on November 30. The general ordered a frontal assault, and, although Hood's army carried the battle, his losses were heavy. A few days later, Hood's weakened command suffered defeat at Nashville and was forced to begin a withdrawal toward Alabama. Once again Forrest was called upon to demonstrate his military efficiency by covering the retreat.

Hood's adventure was the South's last desperate bid to pluck victory from defeat. Sherman was marching across Georgia, and Grant was steadily pushing General Robert E. Lee back in Virginia. The remainder of the war was anti-climactic. In March of 1865 Forrest was promoted to lieutenant general and given command of a theater which included Mississippi, eastern Louisiana, and west

Tennessee. Early in April, he was defeated at Selma, Alabama, but successfully eluded capture. Meanwhile, on April 9, Lee laid down his arms in Virginia, and that was followed a week later by the surrender of General Joe Johnston to Sherman in North Carolina. This left Forrest in command of the last organized Confederate command east of the Mississippi River. Aware of the futility of further resistance, the "wizard of the saddle" surrendered on May 9 at Gainsville, Alabama. As was the case with Lee and Johnston, Forrest and his men were paroled and allowed to go home unmolested.

Bedford Forrest returned to his plantations in northern Mississippi at the end of the war. After four years of inattention, his estates had fallen into disrepair and much rebuilding was required. Ironically he accepted a former Union officer as partner in the operation of the plantation. For several months he lived under the threat of prosecution. In 1864 a federal grand jury had indicted him for treason, and a congressional investigation of the Fort Pillow affair contributed to inflaming passions in the North for a quick trial. The date was set for September, 1866. Friends urged Bedford to flee the country, a suggestion he rejected, although he did secure counsel for the impending trial. For reasons not entirely clear, the case did not reach court, and President Andrew Johnson pardoned Forrest in 1868. That same year he sold his holdings and moved to Memphis.

Although he did not originate the movement, Forrest was apparently one of the early leaders of the Ku Klux Klan. In 1866 he was named the first *Grand Wizard of the Invisible Empire,* but the extent of his participation in that organization is not known. It was said that when the Klan turned to violence, he sought to disband it and, when that failed, abandoned his role in it. When Congress investigated the Klan, Forrest was called to testify. Although he admitted some connection with the organization, he successfully parried the questioning; consequently the extent of his role remained obscure.

After his move to Memphis, Forrest became the president of a new railroad, the Selma, Marion, and Memphis. Construction began, but the enterprise went bankrupt and collapsed following the nationwide panic of 1873. After the collapse of the railroad venture, Nathan Bedford Forrest struggled with debt and declining health. He suffered from chronic dysentery, and his body began to waste away. On October 20, 1877, Forrest died in his 56th year. He was buried in his uniform in Elmwood Cemetery, a quiet resting place for such a flamboyant soldier.

Despite his almost total lack of military experience and training, Nathan Bedford Forrest was a superb field leader. His campaigns have been studied by later military authorities, and his strategy and tactics were employed successfully as late as World War II and the Korean war. Forrest was not without faults. He was not a good subordinate and often quarreled with his superiors, especially when he regarded actions taken by them as revealing ineptness, inefficiency, or incompetence. He expressed his opinions frankly, and sometimes brutally, and that perhaps explains why Confederate authorities initially failed to recognize his abilities and to delegate greater responsibility to him. Thus it can never be known whether he could have succeeded as well with a larger command. Forrest also exhibited a recklessness by becoming personally involved in combat; his death could have had disastrous results for his command. There likewise were occasional mistakes in strategy and tactics, but his many successes tend to obscure those few errors.

Forrest's strategy and tactics were based on his dictum, "get there first with the most." He meant simply to strike quickly with a superior force, although more often than not his command was numerically inferior. Forrest was not, as has been generally assumed, a "hit and run" raider such as Jeb Stuart and John Morgan. Rather he applied the principle of "deep penetration." He sent his forces far behind enemy lines, occupied an area temporarily, and kept the enemy off balance while he meticulously destroyed communications and supplies. His army was not cavalry but mounted infantry; he used horses only for rapid mobility. He was offensive-minded by nature, and invariably kept the enemy confused by attacking on the flanks, from the rear, or at otherwise vulnerable points. His organization was efficient, and, although he could extemporize when necessary, his operations were planned in detail well in advance of implementation.

Finally, Forrest had more effective discipline and higher morale than any other Confederate leader. His punishments for violations were often severe; once he even performed an execution for cowardice himself. Fear was therefore an important component of his discipline, yet he had less difficulty than others in recruiting and granted wholesale furloughs without fear of mass desertion, a move few Confederate generals could take with confidence. The *espirit de corp* in his command was unmatched on either side during the Civil War. Of the 22 highest ranking generals in the Confederate army, all but three were graduates of the United States Military Academy at West Point. Two of the remaining three came from well-to-do families, were well educated, and had some military training. Forrest was the only one who had no military background. That he rose to the rank of lieutenant general was remarkable, but he was a remarkable man.

SUGGESTED READINGS

Nathan Bedford Forrest has been the subject of several largely sympathetic biographical studies. The earliest, authorized and approved by Forrest and published in 1868, is Thomas Jordan and J. P. Pryor, *The Campaigns of Lieut. Gen. N. B. Forrest, and of Forrest's Cavalry* (Dayton: Press of Morningside Bookshop, 1973). That work is limited in the main to Forrest's military exploits, as is an account written by a soldier who served in Forrest's command, John Allan Wyeth, *Life of Nathan Bedford Forrest* (Dayton: Press of Morningside Bookshop, 1975, first published in 1899). Wyeth's biography was also re-printed as *That Devil Forrest; Life of General Nathan Bedford Forrest* (New York: Harper, 1959). Two more recent studies, valuable for exploring Forrest's life before and after the Civil War, are Andrew N. Lytle, *Bedford Forrest and His Critter Company* (New York: Minton, Balch, 1931; reprinted, Putnam, 1947; revised ed., McDowell, Obolensky, 1960) and Robert Selph Henry, *"First With the Most" Forrest* (Indianapolis: Bobbs-Merrill, 1944). There are a number of articles about Forrest, most of which examine specific battles, but two are especially useful in evaluating him as a military leader: William D. McCain, "Nathan Bedford Forrest: An Evaluation," *Journal of Mississippi History* XXIV (1962), 203-225 and Jac Weller, "Nathan Bedford Forrest: An Analysis of Untutored Military Genius," *Tennessee Historical Quarterly* XVIII (1959), 213-251. There are a large number of works which chronicle the Civil War in the West and are useful for examining Forrest's role in relation to the total war effort.

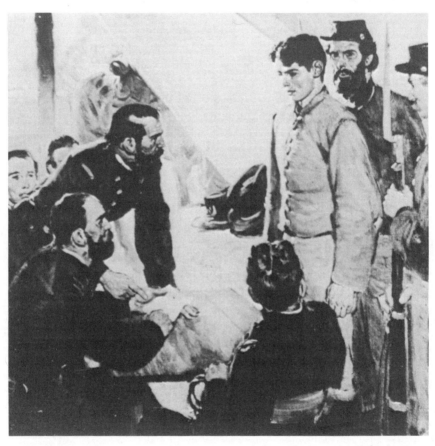

Sam Davis pictured standing before General Dodge. *Courtesy Sam Davis Home Museum.*

8

SAM DAVIS
by Billy M. Jones

S am Davis, a soldier viewed by his Union captors as "too young to die," spread an immortal legend across the pages of Tennessee history by his heroism. Called by some the "Boy Hero of the Confederacy," by others the "Immortal Scout," Davis earned his place in history by choosing to die on the gallows rather than to betray a friend or break his oath as a Confederate soldier. He was but 21 at the time, a mere youth with a lifetime of happiness, adventure, and achievement before him. A tragic waste! But then, wars always tend to claim the bravest and brightest of a nation's youth, for it is by their valor that wars are driven. And the bravest, by their daring too frequently are exposed to the hazards. So it was for Sam Davis.

Sam Davis was a native Tennessean, born October 6, 1842, in Rutherford County, Tennessee, the first son of Charles Lewis and Jane Simmons Davis. His parents were Virginians whose ancestry dated to 1712 in Middlesex County. They were products of their past—and victims of the times. Charles Lewis Davis was born in 1799, married Margaret Saunders in 1824, and settled down, as his father before him, to the life of a tobacco farmer in Mecklenburg County. A comfortable home, good breeding, and community respect made his existence both rewarding and happy until the inevitable march of time put its mark on him. Tobacco culture left his land tired and unreplenished; productivity declined and the land needed rest. There was time but no sure technique, and he grew increasingly uneasy about the future of the soils.

Others had faced his dilemma and had chosen to leave Mecklenburg County for Tennessee. And word had filtered back that land there was abundant and cooperative. Accordingly, in the summer of 1825, Charles persuaded Margaret to move "out west," and they took their belongings and young son along the wagon routes to the settlements in Middle Tennessee, joining others from Mecklenburg County near present Smyrna.

Several years, three more children, and numerous cleared acres later, Charles again was a prosperous farmer with thoughts of building a house equal to that which he had left in Virginia. Then tragedy struck. In late December of 1840 or early January of 1841, his beloved Margaret died after a brief illness. Left now with the responsibility of farm and children without a helpmate, he struggled on alone for a few months, then on May 19, 1841, married Jane Simmons, a younger woman who also had moved from Mecklenburg County. Sam Davis was the first born to that union. Although Charles and Jane would give life to three more children, none of the eight in the Davis household was as endearing as Sam.

From early age he showed signs of sturdy independence and a sense of responsibility beyond his years. He was good natured, quick to learn, and readily accepted by his older brothers because of his willingness to shoulder his share of the chores. His loving nature he inherited from Jane, his ingrained confidence and lack of fear from Charles. And as he grew to manhood, he developed his life happily, balancing a love of riding, hunting and fishing against his farm responsibilities and schooling, first at Stewart's Creek Seminary and later at Walnut Grove. His highest possession was a grey horse, which he named War Bonnet, given him by his father.

All too soon he was 18 and the ugly clouds of civil war hung ominously over his future. His parents encouraged him toward college, and he agreed to attend the Western Military Institute in Nashville. The school had a good reputation and was headed by General Bushrod Johnson and Edmund Kirby Smith, both of whom later would distinguish themselves in the Confederate Army. In the fall of 1860, Sam began his studies in literature and soldiering, just a few months away from that April, 1861, countdown to open conflict between the states.

Young Sam, ever the patriot, could not resist the call to arms. At the end of April he left school to return home, where he announced to his parents that he had joined the Rutherford Rifles, then being formed in the county by Captain William Ledbetter of Murfreesboro. He was described at the time of his enlistment as striking in appearance, six feet two inches tall, with dark hair and dark, shining eyes, and "an air that was commanding yet dignified and gentle; he looked every inch a noble youth."

Once training was completed, the Rutherford Rifles became Company A of the First Tennessee Infantry, and were sent to General Robert E. Lee's command in western Virginia, where at Cheat Mountain the unit first came under fire. Later the Rifles were assigned to Stonewall Jackson's brigade and helped drive Union forces back across the Potomac in the wintry months of 1862. Davis' role in these actions was enough to complete his seasoning and make him battle hardened.

By 1863 Union successes in the West threatened the supply lifeline of the Confederacy. Fort Donelson fell in February 1862, and Federal troops moved up the Cumberland River to occupy Nashville. Then, following the Battle of Shiloh in the spring, Union forces drove to Corinth, Mississippi, capturing and controlling vital railway linkages between those two cities. It became critical to the future conduct of the war for the North to maintain control of the railroads, and General Grenville Dodge, given the charge to protect them, established his command headquarters at Pulaski, Tennessee, some 80 miles south of Nashville on the L & N Railroad.

As the danger to Tennessee had grown worse in 1862, the Rutherford Rifles were ordered to return home, and did so in time to participate at Shiloh. Sam Davis distinguished himself in that battle and suffered wounds from which he recovered. Then, to counter General Dodge's build-up at Pulaski, Confederate General Braxton Bragg ordered General B. F. Cheatham to form a new company of volunteer scouts, to be his "eyes and ears" and help determine the purpose of General Dodge's massive build-up. Cheatham entrusted the command and selection of the scouts to Captain Henry B. Shaw. Sam Davis was chosen from among other volunteers because of "his coolness, daring, and power of endurance." He was chosen also because Shaw had seen him under fire, and because he had known the boy most of his life.

To complete the deception, Shaw assumed an alias—Dr. E. Coleman, an herb specialist—and established himself at Campbellsville, just 15 miles northwest of Pulaski. From there a few brave "spies" were dispatched to gather all available news about Union operations in Nashville and about Dodge in Pulaski. Many of the scouts lived in the open countryside, sleeping in thickets and being fed by patriotic and devoted Confederate women by night. One mingled as a firewood peddler among citizens and soldiers in Nashville; another attended military social functions as a civilian and talked openly with enlisted personnel; still others hid themselves from the lines of march as Union troops were being moved, and relayed accurately the numbers in each unit to Shaw. There also were the inevitable rumors about a beguiling female who deceived a young Union officer and obtained valuable information which she passed along to one of the scouts. Of these scouts, Sam Davis was reported to be one of the most poised and daring, a young man of character, integrity, and patriotism—which made him capable of enduring any privation or peril. He, too, proved exceedingly effective in gathering data. Summed up, the total mass of information was enormous and, as it was to prove later, unbelieveably accurate as to the number, location, and strength of Union forces in Middle Tennessee.

Once amassed, the evidence pointed clearly to a build-up of forces aimed at Chattanooga. Dodge's concentration at Pulaski, in addition to protecting valuable railroad connections, was a major reinforcement effort to General U. S. Grant's impending drive on Chattanooga. Periodically Shaw supplied General Bragg at Chattanooga with some of the information and it proved so accurate that some minor Union operations were embarrassingly thwarted. Dodge became convinced that spies were responsible, and in time word circulated that Coleman was master-minding the clandestine operation. No one seemed to know Coleman or any of his "scouts," so effective was their deception.

To stop the free movement of these scouts in general and to apprehend the culprit Coleman in particular, Dodge detailed the famous Kansas 7th Calvary, nicknamed the "Jayhawkers," a tough, seasoned troop which prided itself on doing a job well. So thorough were they that they monitored every road, bypass, and river crossing. Within a matter of days, they succeeded too well; most of the scouts were captured and imprisoned at Pulaski.

Meanwhile, Shaw (alias Coleman) and his scouts realized that military operations at Chattanooga were imminent. Sensing the urgent need General Bragg would have for the best available information about his Union enemies, Shaw determined to dispatch one of his riders with all that he had. He would choose, as was the custom, one scout to carry the report, and the rest of them would depart individually for Chattanooga to join Bragg. If the "courier" was caught, only he would be imperiled; the others would have no indicting evidence to betray them. Each knew the custom—and the risks if chosen.

While Shaw compiled his report, Davis enjoyed a welcome, if dangerous, respite from his duties. He was given permission to return home for an overnight stay. Although he knew of the Jayhawkers' actions and of the presence of Union troops in Smyrna, near his home, he nonetheless used his daring and his knowledge of the countryside to make his way successfully to his parents' farm house. He rode his prized horse, War Bonnet, which he had kept with him constantly throughout his military service.

Tying his horse to a large rock, he made his way carefully to the house, rapped gently on a window, and was received with an outpouring of warmth and attention by his parents. They wanted to awaken the children, but he persuaded them not to, explaining that he had but a few hours to stay. Thus they covered the windows with quilts to shield the light as they sat and talked in front of a glimmering fireplace. Father Charles repaired and refitted his much-worn top boots; mother Jane cooked him a light supper on the open hearth. Son Sam spoke of his duties, explaining the hazards if caught, and as if by premonition he even told them what funeral arrangement he desired if fate should be unkind to him. Yet, none of them knew that he would soon steal "out the side door to death on the gallows at Pulaski." Finally, as their visit waned, Jane produced a much-needed coat, an old Union blue coat with cape which she attempted to dye with crushed walnut hulls. It was more or less grey, as were his washed out Confederate trousers.

Early in the morning, after a couple of hours rest, Jane awakened him, and Sam said his good-byes. He rode off to keep a rendezvous with his chief at the home of W. T. Carter, only a few miles from Dodge's headquarters in Pulaski. He spent the night of November 18 there with Shaw, talking extensively with him for most of the next day, and then retired early to allow Shaw to complete his report, which was finished around midnight or in early morning hours of November 20. Shaw first had chosen W. L. Moore to be the courier, but later designated Davis because Moore's horse was overly fatigued and required rest.

Shaw handed Davis the report and a few toilet articles, then gave him careful instructions about the route he should take. He was to start southward, picking his way west of Pulaski, and follow the Minor Hill, or Lamb's Ferry Road, to the Tennessee River. He then would cross the river between Decatur and Florence and make his way south of Decatur and on into Chattanooga. All went well and swiftly until late on the afternoon of November 20 when a small group of Jayhawkers sprang from ambush and surrounded him on Lamb's Ferry Road in Giles County. A tired Sam Davis surrendered, and after being searched, he was led to Pulaski and imprisoned in the jail "at the northwest corner of the square." He was surprised to find others, including Shaw, already incarcerated there.

Sam's captors presented their findings to General Dodge. From the saddle bags came a detailed map and specifications of Nashville's newest fortifications. Additionally, from a hollow beneath the sole of Shaw's boot, several papers were produced which contained information about Dodge's own command and fortifications so accurate that the General was convinced a traitor must exist within his own staff. One of the letters bore the signature of "E. Coleman, Captain Commanding Scouts."

Coleman! General Dodge sensed that the opportunity was ripe not only to capture Coleman but also to uncover the traitor within his midst. On the morning of November 21, General Dodge sent for young Davis, took him to his private office, and informed him of the seriousness of the military charge against him. He was a spy on whose person had been found accurate and damaging information about the Pulaski fortification. First believing Davis to be a young man and thus unaware of the danger he faced, the General stressed the importance of making a full disclosure of the mission and the source of the information he carried. When Davis declined, stating in a respectful and dignified manner that he knew the danger and was prepared to accept the consequences, the General became firmer. He insisted that he be told the name of the person who gave him the information, and declared he was convinced that "someone near my headquarters who had the confidence of the officers" of his staff was responsible. To withhold such information as he knew would result in Davis being tried by court martial and condemned to die. Davis firmly rejected the threat, stating: "If I have to die, I do so feeling that I am doing my duty to God and my country."

Again Dodge pleaded, now in a more fatherly tone, for some way to save the boy's life, but Davis responded that it was useless to talk, for he could not betray the trust reposed in him. The General persisted. Here the boy was, captured within Federal lines wearing portions of a Union uniform (a much faded cap and badly worn top boots), and in possession of secret information. Remain silent and face certain death; identify Coleman and be spared. Sam said calmly, "I won't tell General. You're doing your duty as a soldier, and I'll do mine, if I have to die."

It was difficult for Dodge to give up, for it was hard, "even under war conditions to kill such a boy." Yet he was left with no choice. He ordered the boy returned to the prisoners' compound and called for the convening of a military commission within three days to hear the case. It was sheer irony that Dodge had within the same compound the very man he sought. Captain Henry Shaw was the Coleman who just a few hours before had affixed his signature to the captured letter. No signals passed between Shaw and Davis, although each was constantly aware of the presence of the other. Davis knew that should Coleman be identified as Shaw, the risk dramatically increased that many others, not yet suspected and still at large, could be imperiled at a critical time in the war. Thus Davis gave no indication that he had ever met Captain Shaw.

As each day passed toward trial date, the tension mounted. Shaw must have wondered if Sam would break, for pressure came from almost every Union soldier within the compound. Davis was such a fine person, the type anyone would cherish as a friend. Federal soldiers visited him in his cell, urging him to name the informer and save his life. Almost a constant visitor and comforter was Chaplain James Young of the 81st Ohio Infantry to whom Davis would turn in the end to handle his possessions after the execution. Not even the Chaplain could persuade him to confess.

Finally the day arrived, and in a simple proceeding, the facts were presented against Davis. In defense Davis declared that he was not guilty as a spy but was merely a military courier in uniform with a Southern pass in his pocket. Therefore he should be treated as a prisoner of war. The judges could not accept that view; he was pronounced guilty. The date of execution was set for November 27, 1863, the day after Thanksgiving. Davis had expected to be shot, but the Commission ordered that he be hanged by the neck until dead. It was a humiliating type of sentence, but the young soldier did not flinch or show disrespect to the panel of judges. He accepted his fate with the dignity and resolution which had characterized his entire life.

Then a new countdown began. Many interceded on his behalf, first pleading with Davis without success to save himself, then urging Dodge to find some way to commute his sentence. By Thanksgiving Day, almost everyone tempered the gaiety of that holiday with remorse about what would face them the next day. Chaplain Young drew even closer to Sam, spending long hours talking softly and praying with him. Sam asked the Chaplain to join him in singing "The Promised Land," a hymn he remembered as his mother's favorite. Later that night, he wrote a letter to his mother:

> Dear Mother: How painful it is to write you! I
> have got to die to-morrow morning—to be
> hanged by the Federals. Mother do not grieve
> for me. I must bid you good-bye for evermore.
> Mother I do not fear to die. Give my love to all.
> Your son, Samuel Davis.

In a postscript he asked that he not be forgotten after his death, and told his father that he could send for his remains in Pulaski. There would be a few personal belongings which could be claimed also.

Finally, Friday, November 27, 1863, arrived. Drums rolled, and an escort of soldiers marched to the jail. Trailing them was an army wagon bearing a plain pine coffin only recently constructed. Sam left his cell, and in a final gesture, turned to the other prisoners and saluted them with his manacled hands. He then mounted the wagon and took a seat atop the coffin, where he remained throughout the short journey down the main street of Pulaski to a selected ridge just beyond town. There, with other soldiers forming a hollow square around a large tree, was a scaffold.

Davis stepped down from the wagon, sat briefly on the ground and asked how long he had to live. The prison warden, Provost Marshall Armstrong estimated 15 minutes. Any news from the front? Yes, General Bragg had lost at Lookout Mountain. Davis sighed, "The boys will have to fight the battles without me." Armstrong voiced regrets at what he had to do, but Davis responded only that he felt no resentment toward him. He was only doing his duty. Then Davis took a scrap of paper and wrote a final note to his mother:

> Dear Mother: I have five minutes to live, and I will spend it writing to you. I don't want you to grieve after me. I don't only feel that I am doing my country's bidding, but that all heaven is sanctioning the act I am about to take. I have asked the Chaplain to sing, "On Jordan's Stormy Banks I Stand . . . ."

Suddenly a mounted soldier burst into view, yelling, "Stop the execution, stop!" He rushed up to Sam, waving a paper of pardon in his hand, and adding, "It was not too late yet." He pleaded with him to name his informer and accept a full pardon. With great passion Davis responded, "If I had a thousand lives, I would lose them all here and now before I would betray my friends or the confidence of my informer." This last bit of drama had been staged by General Dodge. At his bidding, the rider had made a last attempt to persuade the boy to avoid the gallows.

Unhesitatingly and unattended, young Sam Davis ascended the scaffold. After a brief prayer by Chaplain Young, Sam announced that he was ready. And as one witnessing Federal officer wrote later, "Thus ended a tragedy wherein a smooth faced boy, without counsel, in the midst of enemies, with courage of the highest type, deliberately chose death to life by means he thought dishonorable."

He was buried in the family cemetery "under the trees that shaded him as a boy." His grave is marked by "a simple shaft of

Italian marble," inscribed "In memory of Sam Davis . . . . He laid down his life for his country. A truer soldier, a purer patriot, a braver man never lived. He suffered death on the gibbet rather than betray his friends and country."

The Confederacy may have failed, but Tennessee survived. And Tennesseans remembered—and continue to remember. Monuments have been erected in his honor in the court square in Pulaski and on the capital grounds in Nashville. In 1930 the state of Tennessee purchased the Davis home in Smyrna, and it is maintained as a permanent shrine to his memory. Perhaps Mary Gramling Braly has left the most fitting epitaph of all:

> He gave all he had—life,
> He gained all he lacked—immortality.

SUGGESTED READINGS

All sources used in writing this sketch of Sam Davis are secondary, many of which have been liberally—and, it is hoped, accurately— referenced. Important monographs include Mabel Goode Frantz, *Full Many a Name: The Story of Sam Davis, Scout and Spy, C.S.A.,* (1961); Harnett Thomas Kane, *Spies for the Blue and Gray,* (1954); and Edythe Johns Whitley's two works, *Sam Davis, Confederate Hero, 1842-1863,* (1947), and *Sam Davis, Hero of the Confederacy, 1842-1863, Coleman's Scouts,* (1971). Shorter treatments are H. M. Hamil, *Sam Davis, The Story of an Old Fashioned Boy,* (1959?); William Thomas Richardson, *Historic Pulaski,* (1913); and William Bethel Romine, *The Story of Sam Davis,* (1928). Two vintage journal articles are Mary Gramling Braly, "If I Had a Thousant Lives—," *Tennessee Historical Magazine,* II (July, 1931), 261-269; and S. A. Cunningham, "Sam Davis," *American Historical Magazine,* IV (July, 1899), 195-209. Finally, Adelaide Connie Rowell's fictionalized account, *On Jordan's Stormy Banks: A Novel of Sam Davis, the Confederate Scout,* (1948), is worthy of mention.

9

CASEY JONES
by James W. Moody, Jr.
edited by Robert M. McBride

*A*t 3:52 a.m., April 30, 1900, the legend of Casey Jones had its violent beginning near the railroad station at Vaughan, Mississippi. It was then that Engineer Jones ran his Illinois Central Train No. 1 into the rear of a freight train and hurtled to his death and immortality. Today Casey's memory—and that of all railroad men—is memorialized in a white frame cottage on West Chester Street in Jackson, Tennessee. A surprising change from the customary pillared mansion or frontier log cabin, the more typical historic site, the Casey Jones Home and Railroad Museum is dedicated to the Age of Steam and the working men who built America's railroads. Its two museum rooms contain railroad memorabilia and equipment, while the five other rooms are furnished very nearly as they were when Casey, his wife, and their three children lived there. It is a period piece of a time which, in many ways, is more remote to us than the antebellum or the pioneer.

How is a folk hero made? When comes immortality? Why was Casey Jones singled out among the locomotive engineers of his and later days? In a year which saw 2,550 railroad workers perish in accidents, why has the story of his collision persisted? Why, for that matter, did the famous wreck occur at all? That he is a genuine hero of folklore is indisputable. Yet it has come as a surprise to many over the years that he existed at all. But he assuredly did, and the author of his immortality was a little black engine-wiper from the roundhouse at Canton, Mississippi.

His name was Wallace Saunders, and he idolized Casey Jones. After the wreck, when Casey's body had been found near his locomotive lying amidst the wreckage of cars of corn and hay, the grieving Saunders gave vent to his feelings of awe and grief in what has come to be known as the ballad of "Casey Jones, The Brave Engineer." Can there be many today who have never heard:

> *Come all you rounders, if you want to hear*
> *A story about a brave Engineer.*
> *Casey Jones was the rounder's name,*
> *On a big eight-wheeler, boys, he won his fame.*

> *The caller called Casey at a-half-past four,*
> *He kissed his wife at the station door,*
> *He mounted to the cabin with his orders in his hand,*
> *And he took his farewell trip to the promised land.*

According to the family Bible, on display at the Museum, Jonathan Luther Jones was born on March 14, 1861, son of Frank F. Jones and Ann Nolin Jones. The place of his birth has never been established; southern Missouri and Fulton County, Kentucky, are variously given. (According to the Census of 1880, he was born in Kentucky in 1863.) While he was yet a lad, the family moved to the little town of Cayce, Kentucky, from whence came his nickname of "Casey." His father was a schoolteacher, and Luther, as he was then known, was the eldest of five children. All four of the Jones boys became railroad engineers, and the symptoms showed up early in young Luther.

Cayce is nine miles east of Hickman, Kentucky, and about the same distance north of Union City, Tennessee. In the 1870s, when Professor Jones and his family moved to Kentucky, Cayce was on what was then called the Mobile and Ohio Railroad, and Luther spent a lot of time down by the water tank watching the engines and admiring the engineers. When he was 15, he went to work for the M. & O. as an apprentice telegrapher, but three years later he achieved his dream and "mounted to the cabin" as a locomotive fireman. The next step and the pinnacle of his hopes was the right side of the engine—as engineer. A yellow fever epidemic provided that opportunity when it struck down many train crews on the neighboring Illinois Central. Sensing that a shortage of engineers would result in rapid promotion for firemen, Casey applied for a job on the I.C., and on March 1, 1888, he was assigned a job firing a freight locomotive between Jackson, Tennessee, and Water Valley, Mississippi.

Casey Jones. *Photograph courtesy the Casey Jones Museum in Jackson, Tennessee.*

Casey's hunch proved a good one. In two years—while he was still in his mid-twenties—he passed his examinations and was promoted to engineer, running between Jackson and Water Valley. During the years that followed, he was called to other divisions of the line as circumstances demanded, and in 1893 he was sent to Chicago where he handled one of the express trains carrying passengers out to the World's Columbian Exposition.

Back in 1886 Casey had married Miss Janie Brady, of Jackson. Her mother ran a boarding house where Casey had stayed between runs and where the young couple lived for a while after their marriage. Janie visited Casey while he was assigned to Chicago, little knowing that he had another love—but this time it was a great handsome freight locomotive on display at the Illinois Central exhibit. It was the latest model, and every time Casey went by to see it he could picture himself blasting through Kentucky and Tennessee at the head end of one of the banana specials from New Orleans.

Love was requited, for when the fair closed, Locomotive No. 638 was assigned to Casey, and he had the distinction of running it light over five operating divisions of the line to Water Valley. It was customary at that time for an engineer to be assigned to a particular locomotive upon which he would lavish personal attention and pride, but it was not usual for the management to permit a single engineer to run a locomotive decorated with bunting for a distance of some 600 miles from the fair. This fact, coupled with Casey's assignment to the fast and exacting service of the Exposition, gives an idea of the regard with which he was held by his superiors. In a day and time characterized by hell-for-leather railroading, Casey was officially reprimanded only nine times. Until the day of his death he was proud of a record which had never seen a passenger or crew member seriously injured or killed. That Casey was a fast roller, there is no doubt. But the record does not show that he was careless. At a time of keen competition between railroads, every effort was being made to reduce schedules in order to attract and keep lucrative mail contracts. A successful engineer had to be a bit of a daredevil, and every trip was an adventure unalloyed with the safety devices of today. "To get her in on the advertised" was the goal of every good engineer, and Casey was better than most. He was doing just that when he was killed.

Headaches and heartaches and all kinds of pain–
They ain't apart from a railroad train.

Casey Jones and his pet, No. 638, worked freights from Jackson to Water Valley until January 1, 1900, when he reported to Memphis for assignment to a fast passenger run on the line between Canton, Mississippi, and Memphis. This was what Casey had been waiting for. It was a better job with more pay and greater prestige, but it meant that his family would have to leave Jackson for Memphis. Mrs. Jones and the three children were planning the move from the little house on West Chester Street hard by the Illinois Central yards and away from the line which had echoed to Casey's six-tone calliope "whipporwill" whistle.

The switchmen knew by the engine's moans
That the man at the throttle was Casey Jones.

He had been working on the passenger run for about 60 days when at nine o'clock on the night of April 29 he brought his train into the Memphis station. Upon his arrival he learned that the engineer who had been scheduled to take Train No. 1—The New Orleans Special—on its run south from Memphis was on the sick list. He learned further that Train No. 1 was running late and that there was no other engineer available to take the train south to Canton. Would he do it? Yes, if he could use the locomotive he had just brought into the station. Casey, it seems, now had another pet locomotive. This time it was a fast-stepping, high-wheeled, tall-stacked passenger engine numbered 382, and this night it sported the newly-installed whipporwill whistle. It has been suggested that Casey agreed to "double out" because high water around Canton had idled him more than he liked during the past few weeks and, with his family planning to join him in Memphis, he needed the extra pay.

After he had some coffee and saw to his locomotive he was ready to couple-on to the New Orleans train, and—as it happened—start his "farewell trip to the promised land." Train No. 1 was scheduled to leave Memphis at 11:15 p.m., but it was not until 12:50 a.m., April 30, that Casey Jones and his Negro fireman, Sim Webb, pulled out of the Poplar Street Station and started "through South Memphis yard on the fly" with 95 minutes to make up during the 190-mile run. The normal average speed was 35 mph, but

Casey would have to average nearly 50 mph. That meant running very fast between stops and meets with other trains on the single track.

The night was murky but, as Casey shouted to Sim, "The old lady's got her high-heeled slippers on tonight!" At Grenada they had made up 60 of those 95 minutes. That left only 88 miles, and, at the rate they were going, they would be in Canton on time.

> Put in your water and shovel in your coal,
> Put your head out the window; watch them drivers roll.

But fate was conspiring against them, for at little Vaughan, 14 miles north of Canton, trouble was developing. Casey knew that he would have to meet and pass several trains at Vaughan, but what he did not know as he hooted his way through the countryside at speeds well over 70 was that an air hose on one of the trains had broken, and the caboose and several cars with locked brakes were stalled on the main track.

Conflicting testimony and years of argument color the circumstances of one of the most famous wrecks in railroad history. As they sped around an easy curve north of Vaughan, Sim Webb suddenly spotted the lights of the stalled caboose. He shouted a warning to Casey and leaped for his life from the locomotive. Casey Jones in a valiant last-minute effort slowed his train from 75 to 25 miles per hour, but with throttle shut, brakes on, and reverse lever pulled back, No. 382 and the New Orleans Special smashed into the other train. Casey was the only casualty, if one regards his immortality as "the brave engineer" and his act of self-immolation as a casualty. At the moment that Casey Jones was flung from the cabin to his death amidst the hay and shelled corn of the wreckage, he took his place in the pantheon of folk heroes.

> Fireman jumped, but Casey stayed on,
> He was a good engineer, but he's dead and gone.

Did Casey Jones have the right to assume that the track would be cleared for him? Did the crew of the stalled freight send out a flagman with track torpedoes, as they claimed? Or were they enjoying a false security in the mistaken idea that Train No. 1 could not possibly make up enough time to put it in Vaughan as scheduled? The final verdict has not been reached except in the realm of folklore, and there his memory is secure.

The wreck cost the Illinois Central Railroad $3,323.75 plus a few dollars in injury claims paid to a couple of passengers, two postal clerks, and Sim Webb, who survived his jump with body bruises. Sim received five dollars. Casey's family back in Jackson received $3,000 from the Locomotive Engineers' Mutual Life and Accident Insurance Association. Casey Jones left a wife, three children, his father and mother, and three brothers, all of Jackson. His body was taken to the residence at 211 West Chester Street. Services were conducted May 2, 1900, at 11:00 o'clock from St. Mary's Catholic Church with interment in Mt. Calvary Cemetery. The official report of the wreck, dated July 13 and signed by A. W. Sullivan, general superintendent of the Illinois Central, said " . . . Engineer Jones was solely responsible for the collision. . . ." So ended, it seemed then, the story of Jonathan Luther "Casey" Jones. But really it had only begun.

Wallace Saunders, the Negro engine-wiper, had a way with songs. The wreck was the talk of the roundhouse at Canton. Whether Saunders adapted his words and music from other sources we do not know, but before long the ballad of Casey Jones began to take form, and he began to sing the stanzas. The song caught on and was repeated until it came to the attention of vaudeville performers Bert and Frank Leighton who used it in their act. There are variations in the several versions which have come down to us, but in 1900 the version which is known best today was copyrighted and published by T. Lawrence Seibert, who claimed the words, and Eddie Newton, who acknowledged the music. The sheet music publisher claimed that the song was "the greatest comedy hit in years . . . the only comedy railroad song." The Southern California Music Company of Los Angeles used the covers of the sheet music to tell the public of its "two big hits"; "Kid You've Got Some Eyes," and "Dynamite Rag," together with a minstrel number, "Hold Me Parson, Hold Me, I Feel Religion Coming On."

By 1913 they were singing a calypso version in Trinidad, and the song went to Europe with the Doughboys. Versions are known in several foreign languages, including Afrikaans. Joe Hill, the I.W.W. agitator and poet laureate of the radical labor movement, created "Casey Jones, The Union Scab," which seems to have had its genesis in the fact that Casey "doubled-out" after completing his normal run that fateful night. In Hill's version, Casey is a strike breaker who "Kept his junk pile running . . . was working double time . . . [and] got a wooden medal for being good and faithful on the S.P. line." Indeed, Comrade A. Belonkon, writing in the Moscow *Literary Gazette,* became incensed at the canonization of a foe of the working man!

Thus it was that as Casey Jones lay moldering, his grave adorned by a little wooden cross, his fame marched on and his memory was made green around campfires and in union halls by folk singers and by college boys. Even Locomotive No. 382 refused to die. It was repaired at a cost of $1,396.25 at the Burnham shops of the railroad near Chicago and returned to service. Renumbered 212, it continued to work passenger trains out of Memphis. Over the years it was rebuilt several times, renumbered as 2012, and finally, 5012. It ended its days in passenger service between St. Louis and Clinton, Illinois, and was scrapped in 1935.

Mrs. Jones continued to rent the house on West Chester Street and lived there with her two sons and daughter for a few years. She died in 1958 at the age of 92. Her last years were spent in a rest home, but in earlier times she was often called upon to attend public functions as the widow of the famous engineer. As a matter of fact, Mrs. Jones was kept busy beginning in 1938 when a memorial to Casey was erected at Cayce, Kentucky, by the Lions Clubs of Fulton, Hickman, and Mayfield. Senate Majority Leader Alben Barkley made the principal address. In the years that followed, she appeared on such radio and TV shows as Ripley's "Believe It or Not," "We the People," and "I've Got A Secret." In 1941 she permitted her name to be used in a patriotic appeal to young people and was rewarded with a certificate of thanks from President Franklin Roosevelt. In 1945 she was the grand marshal of the parade which officially opened the Chicago Railroad Fair and, in a remarkable display of advertising enterprise, she presided at the opening of the Sattler Department Stores "nationally famous sales event, the Bargain Train" at Buffalo, New York, in 1950. For these appearances she never got a dime (except expenses), nor did she profit from the sale of the sheet music.

During this period, Casey Jones had not been forgotten by Hollywood. Hedda Hopper reported that Paramount Pictures was planning a musical movie about him which would star, somehow, Robert Merrill of the Metropolitan Opera and Bing Crosby. Another report of the time had it that Paramount had purchased the film rights to Fred J. Lee's *Casey Jones* with Preston Foster slated for the title role. Finally, in 1958, Casey "hit the screen" but it was in the form of a TV serial which, as it turned out, had little to do with the facts of Casey's life. But community leaders of Jackson turned out for a premiere telecast at the television studios and then enjoyed a buffet supper at the New Southern Hotel. By this time, Casey Jones was much on the minds of the people of Jackson. Indeed, by 1955, civic leaders were observing uneasily the activities of a "certain group" which remained nameless in the newspaper reports, but which apparently was inspired by the Davy Crockett craze, and planned to give Casey—and themselves—the same treatment. Accordingly, the City of Jackson signed a contract with Mrs. Jones whereby the city was given all and exclusive rights to the use of the name Casey Jones for advertising signs, novelties, souvenirs, etc. Mrs. Jones received $100 in return for her signature, but the record does not show that the city ever profited directly in any way as the result of the contract.

The 50th anniversary of Casey Jones' death occurred in 1950. In order to commemorate the event fittingly, the Andrew Jackson Chapter of Dixiana Stampers sought the issuance of a postage stamp in honor of Casey and the railroad engineers of America. D. D. Crocker of Jackson was president of this philatelic organization and was given much of the credit for their final success. The City Commission joined in and endorsed a resolution favoring the stamp and saw to it that the efforts came to the attention of their congressman, Representative Tom Murray, chairman of the House Post Office and Civil Service Committee. In Murray's mind, the stamp would pay "tribute and respect to the railroad engineers and through them to all railroad employees and working men in the country." Soon he was able to announce that the Casey Jones stamp would be issued at Jackson on April 20 in an initial printing of 115,000,000.

The Chamber of Commerce got to work, and Governor Gordon Browning proclaimed April 20 as "Casey Jones Day." Plans were made for special postage cancellation dies and the preparation of first day-of-issue covers for stamp collectors. Highway signs and souvenir cards were prepared. Casey's whistle was obtained from its owner in Missouri, and the citizens were urged to wear railroad caps and red bandannas. "Casey Jones Day" was a great success. Ceremonies commenced in Mt. Calvary Cemetery where floral tributes were placed on the grave, including a rosebush sent as a gift from four Oregon division locals of the Brotherhood of Locomotive Engineers. The parade was more than two miles long, and it was viewed by the biggest crowd ever assembled in Jackson. Mayor George Smith presided at the ceremonies on a platform before the post office. Mrs. Jones and members of her family were there, as was old Sim Webb. The crowd heard addresses by Congressman Murray, Governor Browning, and I. B. Tigrett, a resident of Jackson and president of the Gulf, Mobile, and Ohio Railroad. Altogether, five railroad presidents were there. Conspicuous by his absence was the president of the Illinois Central, who is said to have remarked that his railroad did not make it a practice to celebrate its wrecks.

The next time Casey Jones came to public attention was in July of 1953 at Vaughan, Mississippi, where the celebrated wreck had occurred. The occasion was the erection of a highway marker by the Mississippi Department of Archives and History alongside the newly blacktopped road to Vaughan. The famous whistle was there, but there was not enough air pressure to make it work properly. However, the locomotive's bell had been hanging in the belfry of the Black Jack Methodist Church, and it was tolled for the occasion. It was Mrs. Jones' first visit to the place where her husband had died. Evidently the ceremony was fatiguing to her. After all, she had heard it before, and had been called upon many times to tell her story. At one point she reached out and tugged the coattails of a speaker, "Sit down, dearie. Everybody's said all they can," she said. "Besides, it's suppertime."

In 1955 Mayor Smith stated that he planned a "national museum" depicting the saga of American railroading which would honor railroad men everywhere. He came by his interest in railroading naturally. His father had been a railroad man for 50 years, and his father-in-law had been an engineer on the G. M. & O. Work began immediately on the Chester Street property. New green shutters were added, a picket fence was constructed across the front, and a solid board fence was built along the side and the rear of the lot. The house at 215 was sold and razed to make room for a red brick building which would become a sales room for souvenirs.

Meanwhile, Mayor Smith was searching for one of the principal attractions—a locomotive just like the one Casey rode to his death. Diesel locomotives had almost supplanted steam on America's railroad, but he wrote to roads across the country and finally landed what he wanted. The Clinchfield Railroad had a ten-wheeler which was built from the same blueprints and by the same builders as No. 382. It had been in service until March of 1955 on the Black Mountain Railroad, a North Carolina subsidiary of the Clinchfield. It was purchased for $2,500, a sum described by Mayor Smith as less than its scrap value. The locomotive arrived in Jackson in early March, 1956, after being hauled over the tracks of the Southern Railway and the Nashville, Chattanooga, and St. Louis Railroad at no charge. It was then taken to the G. M. & O. shops there where it was refurbished at that railroad's expense.

Work was proceeding rapidly on the house. Two rooms were set aside to house the museum exhibits, and the remainder were restored to their appearance at the turn of the century. Appropriate furnishings were acquired, and wallpaper was made according to samples revealed during the renovation and donated by Birge of Buffalo, New York. Chairman George Gardner made a public appeal for old railroad passes, time tables, telegraph equipment, oil cans, dining car menus of the period, souvenir rail spikes, railroad money and script, a 1900 upright piano, whistles, lanterns, old railroad clocks and watches, scrapbooks, clippings, photographs, torpedoes, flares, etc. All the collected material would be carefully screened, he said, and those items not used initially would be displayed later as part of rotating exhibits.

During the past two decades, the museum has received national attention. In 1961 the Casey Jones home was included in a traveling exhibit prepared by the National Trust for Historic Preservation. Entitled "Preservation: Heritage of Progress," it consisted of panels depicting the destruction and preservation of houses in the United States and abroad. Casey Jones' house was in contrast to the Vanderbilt's cottage at Newport, "The Breakers." Within the state, the Tennessee Historical Commission has erected historical markers at the Casey Jones Home and Museum and at the Poplar Street Station, in Memphis, in addition to the one at the cemetery.

The home of Casey Jones is a simple frame bungalow with a central hall leading from the parlor to the back of the house. On the right is the bedroom where Casey, Janie, and baby Lloyd slept, and back of that is Helen's bedroom; the little room beyond that was Charles'. To the left, as one stands in the parlor, is a room which was rented out to railroad men and to which Casey's body was brought. It and the room behind it now house the museum collection, which includes the watch and notebook carried by Casey when he died. At the back of the hall on the left is the bathroom with its tin-lined bathtub and toilet with wooden overhead tank. The kitchen contains an iron cookstove, wood box, washboiler, and other appurtenances of the time. There is a wainscoting of vertical tongue and groove with wallpaper above.

Every effort was made to keep the house simple—and to make it the sort of home a working man would have had. The effort has been successful, for it must be remembered that Mrs. Jones was living and available to answer questions about her house. Not many pieces of Jones furniture are on display, but the house is well and adequately furnished according to the period. Even the electric lights hang from drop cords from the ceiling, and until recently when it finally burned out, the light on the front porch was one of those old-fashioned clear glass bulbs with the glass tip on the end. That the house is comfortably heated and air-conditioned does not dispel the illusion of stepping into the turn-of-the-century home of a railroad engineer, the blue-collar aristocrat.

So it is that the legend of Casey Jones was born and nurtured. It is a reflection of the admiration and awe which followed the engineer of a steam locomotive. Here was the idol of generations of American boys—a godlike being who held in check the violent, throbbing, roaring behemoth that pounded its way into the nation's heart and took the breath away with its passing and lifted its call over the horizon.

Blow, hogger, high on the right-hand cushions, aloof as an earl without strawberry leaves, an earl in denim cap and goggles, blow for the grade crossings of remembrance, wind a trump for the yard limits of Bangor and Schenectady, La Junta, Cheyenne, Burlington, Walla Walla, Billings, and El Paso. Blow for green from the signal towers of destiny. Blow down the long vistas of American consciousness and for the order boards of eternity. The horn you wound was one with Roland's at Roncesvalles, one with the bugles of far hunting in ancestral memory. No nobler or more melancholy trump will be winded till Gabriel. And perhaps not then.

SUGGESTED READINGS

The most valuable source for the story of Casey Jones, the growth of the legend, and the development of the Casey Jones Home and Museum are four scrapbooks containing newspaper clippings, correspondence, articles, and other material compiled over a period of many years by H. Leroy Pope, Jackson attorney and Madison County Historian and County Judge. The author acknowledges his indebtedness to Judge Pope for the use of the material and to Mayor George Smith and Mrs. Martha Gilland, of Jackson, for their assistance.

Useful secondary source material includes Carlton J. Corliss, *Main Line of Mid America: The Story of the Illinois Central* (New York, 1950); Fred J. Lee, *Casey Jones* (Kingsport, Tenn., 1930); B. W. Overall, *The Story of Casey Jones, the Brave Engineer,* (Jackson, Tenn. 1956); Robert B. Shaw, "3:52 A.M., April 30, 1900" in *Trains Magazine,* XXV (1965); H. R. Whitaker, "The Man at the Throttle was Casey Jones" in *Kiwanis Magazine,* XXVIII (1963). Other material includes the sheet music collection, Tennessee State Library and Archives, Nashville, and Lucius Beebe and Charles Clagg, *When Beauty Rode the Rails* (Nashville, 1962), 14 (final quote of the article).

Sergeant Alvin York standing on the spot where he won lasting fame. *Courtesy Memphis Room, Memphis-Shelby County Public Library.*

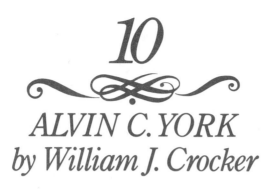

10

ALVIN C. YORK
by William J. Crocker

O n October 7, 1918, Alvin York lay in a muddy foxhole in the Argonne Forest near the little French village of Chatel Chehery waiting for battle orders while German shells burst all around. After instructions came, he later found time to scribble in his battered diary with a snubnosed pencil: " . . . So the order came for us to take hill 223 and 240 the 8th." That order, repeated so matter-of-factly, brought a dramatic change in Alvin York's life. He went into battle on the 8th a faceless infantryman and emerged having accomplished a feat that made him the most celebrated civilian soldier of World War I. In a single action he destroyed a German machine gun battalion of 35 guns by killing 25 enemy soldiers and taking 132 prisoners, including four German officers.

"York, how did you do it?" one general asked after going with him to the spot where the incredible event occurred. It was a question that Sergeant York was to be asked many times, for the enormity of the facts humbles the imagination. With typical self-effacement he responded by giving total credit to God. Through his fervent belief in his God, he felt assured that even in front of the machine guns, as he answered the general, "So long as I believed in Him not one hair of my head would be harmed."

If he had heavenly power on his side, Alvin York also had an earthly upbringing that nurtured in him a fearless character, rifle-accuracy judgement, mental decisiveness, and physical skills that made him a match for that moment in the Argonne.

The upbringing that shaped him was the customs, values, and events of pioneer life in the remote mountain hamlet of Pall Mall, Tennessee, located in the foothills of the Cumberland mountains in the bucolic sounding "Valley of the Three Forks o' the Wolf." This fertile valley, in Fentress County, nestles between seven wooded mountains of the Cumberland range. It was here that Alvin's great-great grandfather, Conrad Pile "Old Coonrod" York, a restless "long hunter" and trailblazer, from a vantage point on one of the mountains one day in the latter part of the 18th century, gazed out over the verdant valley floor and was so struck by its lush calmness that he decided to homestead. The first non-Indian to settle there, he marked off the boundaries of his land. Beside a spring that flowed beneath the rock cave where he first made a bed of leaves and slept, Old Coonrod built a log cabin and set about to prosper through hard work, pioneer tenaciousness, and force of character.

In a converted log corn-crib across the spring and up the mountainside from Old Coonrod's log dwelling, Alvin Cullum York was born on December 13, 1887, the third in a family of 11 children—eight boys and three girls. His mother, Mary Brooks, had inherited 75 acres of the original Conrad Pile estate, as well as a large portion of Old Coonrod's gritty character and stoic will. The flaming red hair that marked the York children came from the Brooks side of the family. Alvin's grandfather, William Brooks, was a red-headed Union soldier from Michigan who had stayed in the valley after the Civil War to marry Nancy Pile.

Alvin's father, William York, who grew up in the valley, was a farmer, blacksmith, and hunter. The blacksmith shop, located in the cave up the mountain from Old Coonrod's spring, sometimes stood unattended while William York went to follow his hunting dogs. Although he never prospered much beyond the necessities of life, William York was so respected for honesty and fairness that his neighbors referred to him as "Judge." Often called on to arbitrate disputes, he also served as official judge of the hotly contested shooting matches in the valley.

The York family was more or less a typical mountain family: large, close-knit, ruggedly self-sufficient, staunchly religious, rigidly disciplined, poor but respectable, community-minded yet fiercely independent, generous with their own kind but suspicious of outsiders, deficient in "book learnin' " but supremely trained in natural lore and survival.

Out of this background Alvin York grew to manhood. Despite the pastoral setting, his was not an idyllic life, for there were many privations. The winters were harsh. There were no doctors. The nearest town was the county seat, Jamestown, "Jimtown" to the local people, 12 miles away over a mountain dirt road. Children had to work at an early age, and Alvin was no exception. From small chores around the house and field work, he graduated to helping his father in the blacksmith shop. His muscles and strength grew apace with his adeptness at shoeing mules and horses. Formal schooling was intermittently held in a one-room building with a single teacher for a hundred pupils, and, although he learned to read and write, Alvin's cumulative class time was equivalent to a second-grade education.

Young Alvin may not have been an eager reader of books, but he was an avid student of the woods. Hunting was a natural pursuit for the mountainman, not only for the practical necessity of providing meat for the table, but also for the joyful diversion it brought from the harsh realities of a hard life. The better a man's hunting and shooting reputation, the more respect he could command, and Alvin had a teacher and a model he could look up to more than all others—William York. In his autobiography Alvin wrote reverently of his father:

> He could follow a trail anywhere, or go through the wildest country on the darkest nights, and never get lost for a minute. He was the best shot in the mountains. Often have I seed him take the centre out of a target, shot after shot. I have seed him fire a dozen times at a target and put most all of the bullets through the same hole.

These were prized skills, and Alvin York mastered them early.

There was nothing the mountaineer enjoyed more than testing his skill with a rifle, and for Alvin the finest pleasure and entertainment that could be had were the Saturday shooting matches. Attracting shooters and their favorite long rifles from throughout the mountains, these contests of marksmanship had strict rules with the prizes being turkeys and steers, sometimes a sheep or pig.

There were two forms of turkey shoots. In one the contestants drew lots for the order of shooting after paying ten cents to stand

and shoot sixty yards at a turkey tied behind a log so that only its head was visible. The shot that hit the head got the turkey. In the other the turkey was staked in an open area 150 yards from the shooter and the shooting was offhand (standing). To count, the bullet had to hit above the knee and below the gills.

The biggest event was the beef shoot. Shots were sold with the price depending on the value affixed to the steer by its owner. There were five winning places corresponding to the two hind quarters, the two front quarters, and the hide and tallow in respective order. Each shooter prepared his own target, a small board with a cross cut in the center by a sharp knife blade. Shooting from 40 yards if using a rifle rest and about 27 yards if offhand, the shooter's object was to "cut the centre," to hit the exact center of the cross. William York was usually called on to measure the gradations from center to decide the winners. Inasmuch as a contestant could purchase as many shots as he wanted, it was possible for one marksman to take all five places and thus "drive the beef home on foot." William York accomplished it more than once—and so did his son Alvin.

The rifle for Alvin York became a tool as specific as language, and the use of it was his poetry. His father by example taught him the care and respect due the long-barreled muzzleloader. Later, when soldier Alvin York was given his first Springfield army rifle, he was appalled at its greasy condition and immediately took it apart and cleaned it. If the German major had known about the Turkey shoots, he might have surrendered his men before they were picked off as they raised their heads above the gun-pits. He would have understood when Sergeant York said, "When I seed a German, I jes' tetched him off."

When his father died in 1911, Alvin, in his early twenties, became head of the family. Already accustomed to hard work, he took any job he could find to earn money. It was during this period of his life—perhaps because of the pressures of long hours of labor together with the natural exuberance of coming into manhood—that Alvin went what the mountain folks called "hog-wild." He began to drink, gamble, fight, and curse. He spent weekdays diligently at work, but every weekend was reserved for drinking bouts and wild shooting sprees with companions from the valley. On the

Tennessee-Kentucky line, six miles from Pall Mall, were the drinking shacks, called "blind tigers," where Alvin and his friends could buy whiskey and find as much trouble as they desired. Although he was a strapping six feet tall, tough as hickory, and loved to drink and fight, Alvin never got into serious trouble.

Eventually, however, through motherly admonitions and pleadings, Alvin began taking long walks in the mountains thinking and praying about his profligate ways. It was characteristic of him to make decisions after deliberate thought and prayer. Finally, the decision he had been edging closer and closer to came during a revival meeting at the Wolf Creek church where his hell-raising apostleship at the "blind tigers" was converted to a fervent discipleship in the Church of Christ in Christian Union. He gave up smoking, drinking, gambling, cursing, and brawling forever. Later in life, writing about this experience, he remembered the exact date of surrender: January 1, 1915. He claimed it was the greatest victory he ever won because "It's much harder to whip yourself than to whip the other fellow."

Once in the church, with characteristic single-mindedness of purpose, Alvin devoted himself to it. He got a job farming with the pastor of the congregation, Rosier Pile, and began a serious reading of the Bible. He helped teach a children's Sunday school class, and with his natural tenor voice and singing lessons, became the song leader for the church. Soon he was being called the "Singing Elder." Temptations to backslide into his old ways were strong for a while, but his will power and self-control were more powerful. Finally he felt completely cleansed, born again. He said, "I felt in my soul like the stormy waters must have felt when the Master said, 'Peace, be still.' "

This was one of the happiest times in Alvin York's life. Although he worked from sunup to sundown and gave his spare time to the church, he felt at peace with himself and with the world. Walking under the stars, he said he wanted to linger on the hillside and "put my arms around themthere hills." And there was a girl now. Little Grace Williams, who had lived unnoticed just around the mountain from Alvin all her life, suddenly was 16 and grown up. Alvin began to watch her at church. Shy and bashful glances grew to chance meetings deliberately planned, and finally to clandestine rendezvous on a winding, shady lane between their houses. Although Gracie's parents were against the courtship, thinking Gracie too young for the 27-year-old Alvin, Gracie was for it. So it progressed—to Alvin's joy.

If there was peace and love for Alvin in the "Valley of the Three Forks o' the Wolf," there was a war raging in other parts of the world. News of it had hardly seeped into the mountains when Alvin received in the mail a red card telling him to register for the draft. He did not know that German battalions were only 65 miles from Paris, mauling the French and British, but he did understand that the red card had come crashing into his sunny day like a threatening thunder clap. His peace was shattered. The storm that ensued was a conflagration of conscience, for Alvin had to struggle with himself before he could do battle against the Germans.

One side of the crisis was his personal opinion that war was wrong and his firm religious conviction that the Bible forbade killing. "Thou shalt not kill" was a commandment to be followed literally. The opposite side of the conflict was his strong sense of national pride and military tradition. His two grandfathers had fought for the Union, and the use of a rifle had been revered in his family from Old Coonrod Pile to him. He had a duty to his country.

Being a man of such sincere and deep convictions, his crisis of conscience was more than a skirmish. He walked the mountains and prayed; he reread his Bible; he talked with Reverend Pile and they prayed together; but there was no refuting "Thou shalt not kill." Between God and country, he felt he had to choose God. Consequently, when Alvin registered for the draft at the local board he claimed exemption by writing on the paper, "I don't want to fight." A few weeks later he made a more formal application requesting discharge from the draft because he was a member of a recognized religious sect whose creed and principles forbade participating in war of any kind. The local board denied the request. Saying that he "couldn't accept the written word of man against the written word of God," he appealed the decision to the district board in Nashville. This time, along with his application, he included an affidavit from Reverend Pile vouching for the anti-war beliefs of the Church of Christ in Christian Union. The appeal was denied.

Alvin became more troubled, finding it hard to believe that

Christian men would defy the word of God and send him to kill. Thinking there might have been a mistake, he appealed to the district board once again. The third and final notice of denial for conscientious objector status was mailed to him on October 6, 1917, one year and two days before he attacked the German machine-gun nests in the Argonne.

When he was called to report to his local board for a physical examination on October 28, 1917, he went because he not only felt it was futile to resist, but also because he had never run from anything in his life. There was no question about his physical fitness: a tightly muscled 170 pounds on a six-foot frame, mountain climbing stamina, and the sharpest eye in the valley.

Less than a month later he was inducted into the army at Jamestown, and sent to Camp Gordan, Georgia, for training. Although sick in spirit, he was determined to obey all orders, praying that he would be shown God's will. The three months of bootcamp were, if anything, easier than the regimen of work Alvin was used to. But the mental and spiritual turmoil intensified when he was transferred as a rifleman to Company G, 328th Battalion, 82nd Division. He knew he was soon to be shipped overseas.

At this point, Private York went to the captain of his company, E. C. B. Danforth, Jr., and earnestly explained his feelings about war and killing. Convinced by Alvin's sincerity and honesty, Captain Danforth took him to see Major George E. Buxton who not only explained the avenues for service open to a conscientious objector, but also tried to show Alvin the purpose and righteousness of the war against Germany. The three men sat in Major Buxton's quarters and engaged in a calm philosophical and Biblical seminar. For most of Alvin's Bible verses condemning killing, Major Buxton was able to quote verses that sanctioned it. The Tennessee mountaineer private was impressed with the New England sophisticated major's knowledge of the Bible as well as with his arguments—in fact, he would later name a son George Edward Buxton York.

But now, although he was swayed by the new evidence, he still wanted conclusive proof. He needed time alone to think and pray and the only place to do that in the right way was in the Valley of the Three Forks o' the Wolf. He asked for and was granted a 10-day furlough. It was on this leave that Alvin York went to a secluded spot on a mountainside one afternoon, knelt, started praying, and prayed through the night and into part of the next day. He came down at peace with himself and his God and announced to his family, "I'm going." He told them he had been assured that he could go to the war and come back to them as long as he believed. Before he returned to his regiment he had more than divine assurance of safety; he had another pledge that swelled his heart with happiness—Gracie Williams promised to marry him when he returned from the war. Although doubts still assailed him when he got back to camp, Alvin never wavered in his faith, least of all during the episode in the Argonne, for he had been to the mountain.

On May 1, 1918, the 82nd division shipped for France. After weeks of drills and hiking the new troops were finally sent into the front lines at Rambucourt on June 26. On the way, seeing the deserted trenches, the gun emplacements half full of water, and the graves marked with wooden crosses, the fresh recruits knew the war was for real. Rambucourt was a quieter sector where new troops were sent for "training" before hitting what was referred to as "No Man's Land." The month of July was spent in a tidal action, going into the line, relieving a division, coming out, then going back in. Throughout this baptism of fire Alvin York felt safe and clung to his faith as tightly as he gripped his rifle.

From Rambucourt the 82nd division joined in the St. Mihiel offensive, the first big concerted American push of the war when General John J. Pershing found out he had a fighting army. As the Germans retreated, Alvin York was on his way to the Argonne Forest, the final phase in the American offensive. On October 4th his battalion reached the Argonne and camped in the woods, where the bloody salient had begun nine days before. Each day, as they were brought up closer to the front, he noticed the growing desolation of the shell-torn trees and the ground furrowed by explosions. Marching even closer, they stumbled over dead horses and dead men. Although the machine guns could not reach them yet, the artillery fire became constant and deadly. On October 7 it was raining as they dug in, waiting for orders.

When the orders came on the 8th to secure hills 223 and 240 and use them as jumping off points to cut through the German line and take the Decauville railroad, the north-south supply line of the

Boche two miles ahead, York's company, wet from a steady drizzle of rain and wearing gas masks in the mustard-fumed air, moved out in early morning darkness, floundering blindly toward their attack position.

The assault was set to begin at 6:10 a.m. A promised artillery barrage to support them did not materialize. Instead the Germans had spotted them at daybreak and poured in their own artillery, inflicting heavy casualties. Between the American contingent and their objective, the Decauville railroad, was a division of German machine gunners securely entrenched on the thickly wooded ridge-tops of three hills that formed a small valley the assault troops would have to cross. The plan was to attack in two waves with split platoons. Alvin, having been promoted to corporal, was a squad leader in the far left platoon in the second wave. He watched the first wave attack and get shredded, enfiladed from three directions, pinned down by bullets and mortars.

Seeing the suicidal futility of a frontal attack, the leader of Corporal York's platoon decided to try a highly risky flanking action to get behind the enemy position and create enough confusion to divert some of the withering fire. Sergeant Bernard Early with three squads, including Corporal York's, was sent to the extreme left. The other two squad leaders were Corporals Murray Savage and William Cutting. Alvin York never forgot the names of the thirteen privates that went along and listed them in his autobiography in this order: Dymowski, Weiler, Waring, Wins, Swanson, Muzzi, Beardsley, Konotski, Sok, Johnson, Saccina, Donohue, and Wills. There were seventeen American soldiers going to flank a German division.

Filtering single file through thick brush, they curled around the left point of the valley until they were about 300 yards beyond their own front lines. At this point they were close enough to the far left ridge to hear clearly the deadly muttering of the machine guns. In a huddled conference some of the men wanted to attack then, but they decided to keep moving farther behind the enemy lines and launch as assault from the rear. Stealthily advancing, they suddenly flushed two German stretcher-bearers who fled through the brush. A few shots were fired to no avail. The Americans, with Sergeant Early in the lead, scurried after them to prevent an alarm

being given. Presently the doughboys, coming through dense un-
derbrush, jumped across a small stream and, to their astonishment,
into the middle of an even more surprised German command post.
The 15 or 20 assorted orderlies, stretcher-bearers, and runners,
including a major and two other officers, bewildered by the sudden
intrusion, threw up their hands in surrender.

As the prisoners were being secured, the German gunners on
the hill above saw what was happening. The prisoners fell flat as the
gun crews jerked their guns around and sprayed the group below.
In the first fusillade six Americans were killed and three badly
wounded. The others either huddled against the prisoners for protection or jumped behind trees. Alvin York was caught out in the
open alone and to the left front of the riddled tableau of prisoners
and captors. From a prone position he began firing at the gunners
who were about 25 yards away, the same distance as the knife
marked targets would have been in a valley shooting contest. Later,
he wrote: "I knowed that in order to shoot me the Germans would
have to get their heads up to see where I was lying. And I knowed
that my only chance was to keep their heads down. . . . Every time a
head come up I done knocked it down."

When he stood to fire offhand, his favorite position, a bold
German officer led a suicide squad of five men in a counterattack.
With fixed bayonets they charged down the hill in single file thinking the shotmaking wizard before them had only a rifle with a five
clip magazine. Not only did their nemesis have in reserve a Colt .45
automatic pistol, but also he had the amazing presence of mind, the
steel courage, and the pinpoint accuracy to kill the sixth man first,
then five, four, three, two, and finally the leading officer—the way
he had learned to shoot wild turkeys. Such a tactic kept the back
ones from stopping to shoot en masse after seeing their leader fall.

This done, Alvin York went back to skull splitting with his rifle
and, between shots, demanding surrender. Hearing the surrender
demand, the captive German major, who had once worked in
Chicago, stood, as York later reported, and yelled, "English?" The
corporal replied, "American." The major said, "Good Lord! If you
won't shoot any more I will make them give up." He did so by blow-
ing his command whistle with great dispatch and ardor after the
steady hand of the sharpshooter aimed the automatic pistol at his
head. With the storied discipline of the German military machine

(and surely with inward relief) the enemy gunners descended with hands up. One, however, concealed a grenade, threw it, and missed. The automatic pistol did not.

With Corporal Savage dead, Sergeant Early and Corporal Cutting wounded, Corporal York was now in charge. He gathered his men and lined the approximately 80 prisoners up by twos, spacing his healthy men along the line. He marched between the first two captives with the German major in front being nudged along by the pistol in his back. The German prisoners were forced to carry the American wounded. At one point, having seen so few American uniforms, the major suspiciously asked Corporal York how many men he had. The corporal replied, pushing the pistol a little harder against the major's back, that he "had a-plenty." When the major attempted to lead the skilled woodsman in the wrong direction, the corporal shrewdly chose the opposite way—directly through the German trenches toward American lines. The surrender scene was repeated at each position with the machine gunners swinging their guns around to fire but instead yielding to the shrill call of the major's whistle. Alvin York and his crippled band ended up with 132 prisoners back at regimental headquarters.

When the facts of the story were corroborated, official heads shaking in disbelief and awe, Corporal York was given a battlefield promotion to sergeant. As it turned out, Sergeant York had produced and directed a small scale rehearsal of a play that was to be performed by the whole German army one month and three days later. On November 11, 1918, the war ended. It was all over but the shouting.

And the shouting for Sergeant Alvin York was long and loud. The news of his heroism spread division by proud division, nation by nation. The honors and the eulogies came in abundance. Marshal Foch, Supreme Commander of Allied Forces, decorating him with the French Legion of Honor, said, "What you did was the greatest thing accomplished by any private soldier of all the armies of Europe." He was presented the French Croix de Guerre and the Italian Croca di Guerra. General John J. Pershing, Commander of American Forces, praised him as "the outstanding civilian soldier of the war." He was given the Distinguished Service Cross and, later, the Congressional Medal of Honor.

American newspapers headlined his miraculous story, and the

nation was ready to pay homage when he returned. New York City showered him with a rousing ticker-tape parade. At the capitol members of congress stopped the nation's business to greet him with a cheering standing ovation. Journalists clamored for interviews. Entrepreneurs and promoters, including Florenz Ziegfeld, offered him huge sums of money to go on the stage, into movies, and to endorse commercial ventures.

Such a whirlwind of goings-on and fancy to-do's was as foreign to the tall, raw-boned, freckle-faced mountaineer as France had been. He neither desired nor was prepared for fame, but he handled it with the natural grace and uncanny good sense that marked all his actions. Always in control of himself and his situation, whether facing a battalion of machine guns or a battery of knives and forks, he said of an elaborate banquet in New York, "I didn't know what all the plates and knives and forks and spoons were for. So I kinder slowed up and jes' kept a couple of moves behind the others. So I knowed what to do." One officer said of the sergeant that he seemed always to do instinctively the right thing.

The adulation embarrassed him. The decorations he accepted simply as a soldier who had done his duty; the offers of wealth he refused, saying with customary economy and straightforwardness, "Uncle Sam's uniform ain't for sell." Although he appreciated the honors and treated the demands on his time with smiling forbearance, the only glory he really wanted was to be among his own people in the Valley of the Three Forks o' the Wolf, the tiara of the Cumberland peaks his only crown. The farm boy had seen Paris, but there was no doubt in his mind where he wanted to be.

The valley was ready for him. On the mountain trails the reception was quiet in comparison to Paris boulevards and New York avenues, but the neighbors' hands, the family smiles, and a mother's tears were the only welcome that mattered. The first thing he did was to go hunting—for Gracie. Next, he went to the mountainside where he had prayed for guidance. He knelt again and gave thanks. "In a few days," he said, "I had the old uniform off and the overalls on. I done cleaned up the old muzzle-loader. It was all over. I was home."

He was home, but there was a difference. He was famous. He and Gracie were married in the valley, but the governor of Tennessee came to perform the ceremony amid thousands of people. He remained a farmer, but on 400 acres of land, much of it the original Conrad Pile homestead, in a new house with modern facilities—all bought by a public subscription fund arranged by the Rotary Club in Nashville. Tennessee gave him a "day" in Nashville where he was presented with gifts from clubs and communities throughout the state. He was besieged with requests for personal appearances and speaking engagements.

After the public acclaim subsided, Alvin York had time to assess what had happened to him. From the 82nd "All-American" division, a hodgepodge of nationalities and religions, which Alvin approached first with feelings of alienation, then respect, then acceptance, and finally love and battle kinship that he described as "sort of clear, like a fire of pine logs on a frosty night," to the status of national hero and world celebrity, a span of little more than a year, his uncomplicated life of mountain isolation had undergone a series of explosive breaches:

> Before the war I had never been out of the mountains. I had never wanted to be. I had sorter figured that themthere mountains were our shield against the iniquities of the outside world. They sorter isolated us and kept us together so that we might grow up pure-blooded and resourceful and God-loving and God-fearing people. They done that, too, but they done more'n that. They done kept out many of the good and worthwhile things like good roads, schools, libraries, up-to-date homes, and modern farming methods. But I never thought of these things before going to war. Only when I got back home again and got to kinder thinking and dreaming, I sorter realized hit.

With this realization and the belief that his worldly experiences had been God's way of preparing him, he began another fight, a lifelong battle to bring progress and education to his beloved valley.

The first thing he did was to get a modern road built through the mountains, now called the York Highway. Next he began his master project, an up-to-date school in Fentress County. With his own money, plus aid from the county and state, the plan was put into motion. To help, he agreed finally to write the story of his life, which was published in 1928. Through many obstacles, including the Great Depression, Alvin York stubbornly fought until York Institute, an agricultural and industrial trade school, was a reality.

His fighting spirit was aroused again with the American entry into World War II. Although 54 years old, he was commissioned a major and assigned to duty training infantry. Upset at the rejection, as "illiterates," of a group of mountaineers, he offered personally to train them and lead them into combat. However, bad health forced him to relinquish the idea of active involvement in the war. Instead he contributed a daily column, ranging from inspirational talks to suggestions on methods of warfare, to a Memphis, Tennessee, newspaper, *The Commercial Appeal.* He had become a diligent reader and was well informed of events in all parts of the world.

Sergeant York had been approached many times to make a movie about his exploits, but always refused on religious grounds until 1941—mainly for two reasons: it might help inspire American soldiers, and all the profits would be used to start a project he had always wanted, a Bible school. The movie won Gary Cooper an academy award for his portrayal of Sergeant York.

In 1954 the rugged old fighter had a stroke that left him bedfast. It was the beginning of the end for one of the world's most courageous and generous men, but not before other honors came. On August 21, 1957, he left his house for the first time since his stroke to go to Jamestown to accept an automobile with special wheelchair apparatus from his old division, which had become the 82nd Airborne. Having proclaimed the occasion "Sergeant York Day" in Tennessee, Governor Frank Clement presented him a car tag with the symbols "A-A 82" for the All-American 82nd Division.

There continued to be visitors who wanted to meet the hero, and he spoke out fearlessly on issues of the day until his death in a Nashville hospital on September 2, 1964. His devoted Gracie declined the offer to let the sergeant lie in state at the Tennessee capitol. She took him back to the sun room of his house in the valley. With services at York's Chapel, he was buried with full military rites in the Wolf River cemetery.

Two monuments of note commemorate Sergeant York. A bronze statue sculpted by Felix de Weldon, the artist of the famous Marine Corp memorial of the flag raising at Iwo Jima, stands on the

Tennessee State capitol grounds. The other, a marble headstone erected at the gravesite by "Miss Gracie" and the seven York children, is a 12-foot-high cross that towers over an angel, a stack of books, and a rifle.

Alvin York's story has been told and retold, for it is epic in proportion—and his "log-cabin" background and "folksy" ways have captured the American fancy. His life is the embodiment of the American dream; he is the apotheosis of the American hero—Natty Bumppo with the simple grandeur of Abraham Lincoln. More important, his feet have remained marble. A cynical, anti-heroic, iconoclastic age has not been able to deface or diminish the record of his heroism. His courage, firmly rooted in honest, steadfast character and buttressed by undeviating faith, is its own invincible defense.

SUGGESTED READINGS

There are two books on Alvin York's life. Sam K. Cowan's *Sergeant York and His People* (New York: Grosset and Dunlap, 1922), was the earliest. Besides a biography of York, it presents an authentic, if at times romanticized, description of the customs and manners of the mountain people. The other book, and more valuable, is Alvin York's autobiography, *Sergeant York: His Own Life Story and War Diary* (Garden City, N.Y.: Doubleday, Doran and Co., 1928), edited by Tom Skeyhill. Written in his own idiom, it reflects the flavor of York's life while at the same time revealing the man's sensitivity, common sense, and confidence in his actions. The book includes entries from Sergeant York's war diary, as well as the official affidavits from those connected with the fight in the Argonne. The narrative by Skeyhill of how the book came to be written is not only intriguing in itself but also further revealing of Alvin York's character.

To place Alvin York's Argonne exploit in the wider context of the war, there is no better book than Laurence Stallings' *The Doughboys* (New York: Harper and Row, 1963), a meticulously detailed history of the American involvement in World War I.

Newspaper accounts of York's heroism were set pieces, mostly from the national news services. Through his life there were sporadic items in newspapers and the major news magazines, such as *Time, Newsweek,* and *Life,* about the sergeant's troubles with the IRS. One of the more informative newspaper articles in which Sergeant York expresses his opinions on such issues as the Korean War and Fidel Castro appeared in the August 28, 1960, edition of *The Commercial Appeal* in Memphis.

11

TOM LEE
by Charles W. Crawford

*J*ust as Tennessee's pantheon of heroes includes people of diverse backgrounds, levels of education, races, and social standings, so their qualifications to enter this exclusive group also are varied. Some, like Andrew Jackson and John Sevier, were elevated to this status because of a lifetime of leadership and respect. Others, like Davy Crockett and Daniel Boone, achieved fame because their steadfast adherence to a colorful style of life identified them in the public mind with an enduring aspect of folklore. A creative few, such as Sequoyah, invented previously undreamed of things to make life better for others. But some of Tennessee's heroes led a life generally quiet and inconspicuous except for one crucial day of their lives when they did deeds that have lived beyond them.

It is in this last category that Tom Lee belongs. The first 39 years of the life of this black laborer were lived in an obscurity unrelieved by wealth, education, or position. It was neither leadership nor respected status that made him a hero, but his actions during a short time late on a May afternoon in 1925. After his brief day of heroism, Tom Lee returned to the obscurity of a laborer's job for the remaining 27 years of his life.

Little is known of Tom Lee's early life. Born in 1886 in poor circumstances in Hopefield, Arkansas, a small town across the Mississippi River from Memphis, he grew up to a life of poverty and hard work, the common lot for blacks in the Mid-South at the beginning of the 20th century. He became, according to a later newspaper report, "a roustabout—a jack of all trades . . . when trades for Negroes were pretty limited." His various jobs included labor as a field hand, river roustabout, and levee worker. During this time he married, but his meager earnings never enabled him to acquire a home or any real estate. He developed an interest in gardening, while his wife Margaret's hobby was in raising chickens. More than anything else in life he wished to own "a small cabin." A religious man, he was devoted to the Baptist church, but he was also, according to a reporter's description, "a typical, crapshootin' negro roustabout, who loves his snort of corn licker as well as any man along the Mississippi levees." His manner seems to have been quiet and respectful of others. He later was described by E. H. Crump, Memphis' political boss, as being unassuming and polite. There were no indications in Tom Lee's life that he would ever receive fame and honor.

On May 8, 1925, Tom Lee was working as a levee contractor's helper for the C. W. Hunter Company of Helena, Arkansas. Thirty-nine years old, strong and accustomed to outdoor work, he had been cutting brush for willow mats used by the contractor to build revetments along the river banks. This day, however, he had been directed to take a company official by motor boat to inspect the willow stands along the river. Leaving his passenger at Helena to return to Memphis by train, Lee started upstream alone in a small motorboat belonging to the company. Humorously named for a famous race horse, *Zev,* the skiff was weather-beaten and unpainted, but it was equipped with a powerful four-cylinder Sterling gasoline engine. The *Zev* was 28 feet in length and had a maximum capacity, in addition to the operator, of eight people.

All deeds of heroism must take place in appropriate settings. These commonly are places of battle, crisis, or disaster, where one person's actions can change the course of events. For Tom Lee the setting was the Mississippi River between Helena and Memphis. One of the greatest rivers on its planet, this stream, flowing southward for 2500 miles to the Gulf of Mexico, moved with the weight of the water drained from 1,244,000 square miles of land. From the Appalachians to the Rockies it gathered water from innumerable small streams pouring into more than 40 major tributary rivers, which in turn flowed into the main trunk to make the Mississippi, monarch of North American rivers. Drawn toward the Gulf by the force of gravity, the waters flowed swiftly and with irresistible

Tom Lee. *Courtesy the COMMERCIAL APPEAL.*

power. The river's currents had scoured the great Mississippi valley and upon and underneath its sandy bottom lay human bones and the remains of countless flatboats, keelboats, steamboats, and other vessels which had become its victims. Beautiful and useful, it was also a killer of men and a destroyer of their property.

While Tom Lee was at Helena, the other principal characters in the drama were gathering on the waterfront in Memphis, about 60 miles to the north. They were mainly engineers, with some family members and guests included. The Mid-South division of the American Society of Civil Engineers was holding a convention in Memphis, where the Engineers Club of Memphis had assumed responsibilities for local arrangements. Relations between the two groups were cooperative, plans being under way to establish a local chapter of the American Society of Civil Engineers in Memphis following the convention. Naturally, the local Engineers Club of Memphis wished to extend its best hospitality to members of the convention. The locals had planned a trip down the Mississippi River, including lunch and an inspection of the construction of willow mats used by the U.S. Corps of Engineers as part of its revetment program to prevent caving of the river banks. The inspection was to be made near Carlyle Bend, more than 20 miles downstream from the city. Invitations had been issued to the group by Major D. H. Connolly, District Engineer, and Montgomery Gardner, Principal District Civilian Engineer of the Corps. Two boats were provided: the *M. E. Norman,* belonging to the Corps of Engineers, and the *Choctaw,* belonging to the Dredging District.

It was the *Norman* which was destined to be known the next day to people throughout the nation. She was as modern as the United States Corps of Engineers could make her, yet with her stern paddles and twin smoke stacks she was reminiscent of the great steamboats that had plied the Mississippi during the previous century. A new boat, the *Norman,* had been built one year before at Morgan City, Louisiana, for the M. E. Norman Towing and Lumber Company and had been purchased by the United States Corps of Engineers on January 15, 1925. She was a steel-hulled stern-wheeler with a length of 114 feet and a beam of 26 feet. Originally she drew 3.9 feet of water and was capable of a speed of 12 miles an hour. But the Corps of Engineers had converted her to an oil-burner, vastly increasing her original weight. Two oil tanks, larger than railway tank cars, replaced her original coal-burning system. A one-and-a-half-ton refrigeration unit was installed on the upper deck. Other machinery and fittings weighed the boat down so that only a few inches of freeboard remained, and waves occasionally washed over the main deck. The *Norman's* conversion had been completed only shortly before the engineers' convention. Designed for towing, the vessel previously had not been used for passenger service. The crew included 10 men, in addition to the master and pilot, Howard Fenton. Major Connolly, with these facts in mind, directed that the passenger list be limited to 50 people, presumably a safe number.

The people who filed aboard the *Norman* that Friday afternoon were a varied group, including more than a dozen women and several children. One of the oldest passengers was Mrs. Lydia Hidinger, who was 73. Other older members were Captain C. H. West, a Greenville member of the Mississippi River Commission who was about 70, and Walter K. Stromquist, the city sanitary engineer of Memphis. J. Frank Coleman, a prominent engineer from New Orleans, boarded with his hat clamped firmly on his head and a supply of cigars in his pockets. A young engineer, Charles Okey, and his wife, Lucy, joined the group. They had bought new suits for the occasion; hers included new springs shoes, a hat, and a cape, a garment in style that spring. One of the passengers was a Memphis employee of Morgan Engineering Company, Harry Wiersema, who had an unusual hobby. He was a long-distance swimmer, having participated in the Memphis Fourth of July races which involved swimming to the bridge at the city from a point five miles upstream. Although less experienced than Wiersema, Jack Corthran, the engineer of the boat, was also a powerful swimmer.

Passengers continued to file aboard, some with wives and children in tow. Mr. and Mrs. C. E. Shearer were taking their child of about five on the tour. Mr. and Mrs. Ralph Bosard boarded with their son, Ralph, who was about 10 years old. William Richards, of Memphis, brought his young son. Jim Wood, a hefty Memphis engineer, went up the gangplank with his wife. Several other guests were also part of the group. Among them were a well-trained Boy Scout and a young lady wearing a yellow hat and carrying an umbrella. She was escorted by a dashing army officer.

The officers of the vessel took their places. There was C. G. Hutton, an engineer employed by the Corps, wearing a suit with coat and vest and shoes tightly tied. The captain and pilot was Howard Fenton, 55. Although he had been a river pilot for 21 years, having served on the famous *Katie Adams* from 1906 to 1914, he had never piloted the *Norman* before. Despite the plan to limit the number of passengers to 50, 11 extra persons found their way aboard the boat.

Only one expression of doubt was heard as the boarding was under way. A designer employed by the Corps of Engineers, Arthur D. Marcotte, arrived with his young son to go on the excursion. He had intended to go on the *Choctaw,* and when he found that it had left, he refused to board the *Norman.* Having assisted in the conversion of the new vessel to an oil-burner, he maintained, in claims that later were to cause trouble for him with his superiors, that the *Norman* was unsafe because the specifications had not been followed properly. He insisted that the oil tanks on each side of the boat should have been connected by a pipe so that the fuel would be burned evenly from both tanks rather than by emptying one tank while the other remained full. Because the pipe had not been installed, he feared for the stability of the boat. To the disappointment of his son, he refused to join the tour. Apparently his doubts were not shared by others, however, for the craft was filled to capacity when it cast off at 12:30 p.m. None of those aboard knew that almost a third of their number would not live to see another sunrise.

The trip down the river was uneventful. The passengers ate lunch and watched the muddy banks and green foliage of springtime slip by. Some, looking downward, may have marvelled at the force and volume of the vast current that extended almost a half mile on either side of the vessel. If, from whatever impulse, any had bent and placed their hands in the water, they would have found it surprisingly cold in comparison to the balmy warmth of the spring sunshine. The water should have been cold. Its rush toward the south had begun in the melting snows on the upper elevations of the great Mississippi watershed.

By mid-afternoon the boats arrived at the Pinckney landing on the Arkansas side of the river. While the men went ashore to examine the revetment work, Lucy Okey stayed aboard with her elderly friend, Lydia Hidinger. When they went below during this stop, Lucy Okey noticed that water, which had been breaking across the main deck, was running down the stairs toward the lower level of the boat. Calling one of the porters, she asked, "Boy, does this boat always act this way?" "Ma'am, I don't know," he replied, "but I know they're scared of her." Tom Lee, proceeding upstream, was still several miles below the Pinckney landing.

Returning to the two boats at the landing, the men filed back aboard. The Memphis engineers had scheduled a meeting during the *Norman's* return in order to complete plans to form a local chapter of the American Society of Civil Engineers in their city. As the two boats cast off, men on a government boat tied at the landing noticed that the *Norman* was listing sharply, with one side about three feet higher out of the water than the other side. As the *Choctaw* moved ahead, several of its passengers noticed the list of the *Norman* and the wash of waves over its deck. But there was no alarm on the ill-fated vessel. Captain Howard Fenton, pilot and master of the craft, noticed difficulty in steering, but, as he was inexperienced with the *Norman*, thought that the passengers' unevenly distributed weight was responsible. As the only boat's officer aboard the *Norman*, he apparently felt he could not leave the pilot house to check conditions below. Instead he sent word to the passengers to disperse around the decks rather than to gather in one area. Captain Fenton's instructions caused no alarm. The engineers started their session in a screened-in area of the main deck; the women and other guests were in the front part of the boat. Some were probably beginning to think of the evening banquet awaiting them in Memphis. During this time Tom Lee, moving rapidly up the river in the *Zev,* passed the landing at Pinckney.

Less than an hour after leaving the Pinckney landing, the *Choctaw,* which had been drawing steadily ahead, passed around a bend and out of sight. The *Norman* was alone on the great river with no communications equipment. The boat passed the north end of Josie Harris Island and headed straight upstream against the current toward Coahoma landing. As Tom Lee, moving swiftly in the *Zev,* passed the wallowing sternwheeler and moved on ahead, he became aware of something that the more educated river travelers on the large boat were not. Something was wrong. The *Norman* was in trouble. Now far ahead, he reduced speed to keep the steamboat behind him in sight. The boat was then at a point where the channel was 60 feet deep and the current tremendously swift, reportedly the worst between Memphis and Helena. Eddies and whirlpools swirled in the murky waters.

It was here that trouble struck—slowly at first, then rapidly. The boat, already unstable, gave a sharp list to starboard. The assembled engineers were quickly ordered to move to the high side of the boat, and the Corps engineer aboard, C. G. Hutton, went below to examine the engine room. The assembled passengers, because they already had been asked several times to change position, did so calmly, but Hutton, going below, made an alarming discovery. The entire lower deck was awash. After notifying Major Connolly and Captain Fenton, he was ordered by Connolly to remain in the pilot house to relay any orders.

The pilot then made a belated and difficult decision. Realizing, as the veering and rolling of the boat increased, that it was in serious difficulty, he decided to steer toward the Arkansas bank. As he turned, the rolling of the vessel worsened. Alarmed by the rocking of the boat, Charles Okey, the young Memphis engineer, left the meeting to find his wife Lucy. He found her hurrying in search of him. Together they went to the outer deck, and he noticed that most of the passengers were still calm. They could not believe that the boat would turn over. After all, it was an army boat belonging to the U.S. Corps of Engineers. Besides, it was filled with some of the most eminent engineers in the United States who certainly should know better than to board an unsafe vessel.

If the pilot had shared their confidence, he was losing it rapidly. The sun was sinking below the willow trees, and the cool of night was beginning to descend as he turned the boat toward the Arkansas bank. Then he made a disquieting discovery. The bank on that side of the river rose vertically 15 to 20 feet above the racing current. There was no escape to the west for the passengers. He then decided to run the boat toward the east, or Mississippi, bank of the river. As he spun the wheel to make the turn, the steering mechanism failed. The boat slowed, turned across the current, and came to a stop. It was dead in the water. The low side of the boat dipped under the water line as the onrushing current, with the irresistible weight of the Mississippi River behind it, poured over it, forcing it under. Tom Lee, looking back from far up the river, saw the great vessel slowly roll over under the weight. The smokestacks and superstructure went down. The *Norman* turned turtle.

Seeing the steamboat turn upside down, Tom Lee realized that he would be needed. He turned his skiff sharply downstream. The *Zev* leaped ahead. For the 72 people on the *Norman* there had been little time to act. They could only be cast into the water or be trapped in the boat as it went down. Probably only about 30 seconds elapsed from the time the vessel started turning until it had completely capsized. The elaborate screening of the craft, which protected workmen against mosquitoes while the *Norman* was anchored along the river, made it a death trap for some passengers who were imprisoned on the boat as it sank. But most, being on deck, either jumped or were spilled into the water as it rolled under. No one was in charge of emergency procedures. There apparently was an adequate supply of life preservers, but most were either on top of the boat or stored behind the two smokestacks, where they could be reached only by passing through a narrow door. Although several passengers got life preservers, few had time to put them on before the boat went under.

Most of those aboard survived the capsizing. Captain Fenton, from his position in the pilot house, was one of the first to realize the *Norman* was turning over. Shouting that the boat was gone, he jumped out a window into the water. Before he had the choice of following the captain, Engineer Hutton fell out the window, cutting his leg on a guy wire on the way down to the water. The Okeys had moved to the railing when Okey told his wife they would have to leave the boat. At first, she refused to believe it. He untied her new lace shoes, but she objected to discarding them. It was only when he replied, "I don't think we're going to need them anymore," that she realized the seriousness of the situation. Hearing the crashing of dishes and the falling of the refrigeration units, she incongruously thought of all the food that was going to be wasted. Then they were spilled into the water. One man burst above the surface, gasping for air after he had broken through a window about 10 feet below. The *Norman* was upside down. The passengers who had not been trapped in the boat were scattered in the water around the hull. It was shortly after 5:00 p.m.

Although they were far from the bank and in deep water and swift current, there was still hope. The *Norman,* although upside down, was floating. The shocked survivors began clambering atop the hull and helping others aboard. There was no panic. Forty-five years later Lucy Okey's strongest memory of the disaster was "the wonderful behavior of the people on there. Everybody was trying to do for somebody else." Charles Okey helped drag one or two men and a woman out of the water. L. L. Hidinger, of the Morgan Engineering Company, pulled himself and his son from the water to the upturned bottom of the boat. Then he dragged W. W. De-Berard, the editor of an engineering publication, aboard. Too exhausted to stand up, DeBerard held Hidinger's feet so that he could reach others in the water. Probably more than half of those who survived the capsizing were gathered, just out of the reach of death, on the upturned bottom of the vessel. Then they discovered a new horror. The *Norman* was sinking. Settling stern first, she fell away beneath them toward the bottom of the Mississippi.

Only a few of the passengers in the water were able to swim to safety. Jack Dorroh, the intrepid Boy Scout from Oxford, Mississippi, was the first to reach the Mississippi shore. While on the up-turned bottom of the boat, he had stripped off his clothes and dived into the current. After trying to save a woman, who slipped from his grasp and was lost, he headed for shore and arrived safely. George Foster and one young boy, about nine, were able to reach shore, as was Harry Wiersema, the long-distance swimmer. Some of those in the water saw a remarkable sight: J. Frank Coleman, the imperturbable New Orleans engineer, swam by, hat in place and still smoking his cigar. He also reached the bank. One other swimmer almost made it. C. G. Hutton, who later drifted ashore, reported that Jack Corthran, the steam engineer of the boat, passed him, swimming "like a passenger train" and reached shallow water, where he was able to stand up. Apparently, however, the exhaustion of the swim and the shock of the cold caused him to collapse before he could reach shore, for he was among those who were lost. In all, only about a half-dozen were able to swim to safety. The others drifted, struggling in the current.

That was the scene Tom Lee saw as he piloted the *Zev* toward the spot where the steamer had disappeared. None of those in the water knew that help was on the way. The world of drowning people, like that of soldiers in battle, seems to be one of vivid impressions but limited scope. Few of the victims in the water were aware of anything beyond their immediate surroundings. Some slipped beneath the surface and drowned. The elderly Captain West, having lost his life preserver, struggled in the current, weakening rapidly. Jim Wood, who was able to swim, was having to support his wife as well as himself. The young lady with the yellow hat was helpless in the water. Unable to swim, she had been abandoned by her army officer escort, but, fortunately, she had opened her umbrella and was being buoyed up by the air trapped under it. Needless to say, her escort never again would be a welcome caller at her home. C. G. Hutton, only a fair swimmer, had stayed afloat until he was able to seize two drifting life preservers. He had removed his coat and vest, but his tightly tied shoes resisted his efforts to remove them.

The young couple, Charles and Lucy Okey, found themselves involved in a desperate drama in the water. They had been given two life preservers while they were on the bottom of the overturned boat, but Charles had generously given his to an elderly acquaintance. Although he could barely swim, he had fastened the remaining life preserver on Lucy. They went into the water together, where he tried to keep himself afloat by swimming on his back, but he lost heart after being repeatedly pulled under the surface by the whirlpools in the powerful current. He decided, with his strength ebbing from the cold and exhaustion, to swim away from Lucy to die, saying, "The children need you more than they need me." Seizing him tightly, she replied, "No, if you go, I'll go too." They struggled in the water as he sought to leave, but her strength and determination were the greater. He managed to remove his new coat, which floated away on the current, but before it did, Lucy took his American Society of Civil Engineers pin and fastened it to her dress. They floated helplessly together, cold and becoming weaker. To this point, there had been no shouting or screaming. The victims fought their individual battles with cold and the current quietly, needing every breath they had. Suddenly Lucy screamed. But it was a scream of hope rather than of despair. A man in a boat was coming toward them.

Tom Lee's arrival was timely. The sun was going down, and soon shadows would be gathering over the river. The surviving passengers were scattered more than a mile down the current, exhausted from their efforts and the loss of body heat in the numbingly cold water. Tom Lee did not waste time. Realizing that the *Zev* could easily be swamped, he avoided steering into the midst of the group; instead he approached them one by one. Attracted by Lucy Okey's scream, he reached her first. Gripping her husband with one hand, she was holding a handkerchief in the other to wipe her nose, which was running from the cold and the water. Tom Lee extended an oar, saying, "Lady, throw that handkerchief away so you can catch this oar." As she was pulled toward the boat, she managed to get her husband's chin over the edge of the gunwale and help him in before entering herself. Guided by her yellow hat, Tom Lee saved the resourceful young woman floating with her umbrella. He reached Captain West and seized him just as he had given up the struggle and started to sink. Careful not to overload the boat, he hauled in five others and sped to a sandbar where he let his passengers out in two feet of water, to stagger ashore near Coahoma Light Landing on Cow Island.

Racing back for other survivors, he rescued W. W. DeBerard, who was keeping afloat by holding to three oars that had floated from under a lifeboat as the steamer went down. Al Fry, who was clinging to a piece of timber, was pulled aboard, as were Jim Wood and his wife. Wood was still swimming with one arm and holding her with the other. To Garner Miller, grasping the overturned lifeboat on which his wife was sitting, it seemed that Tom Lee came out of nowhere. Major Connolly and George Foster were also pulled aboard with the same group of survivors. Without saying a word, Tom Lee rushed them to shore so that he could race back for another load.

Tom Lee's courage and calmness were vital. There is no doubt that most of those he pulled from the water would have died without his help. His description after the event was terse:

> I don't know how many folks I pulled out of the water. It wasn't no time for this here counting heads. They didn't lose they heads like a lot of crazy folks I have seen in the water. I guess it's a good thing they didn't or I sure would have

got scared, too. The sensiblest drowning folks I ever saw. Just waited for me when I waved at them, and I catched them in the *Zev.*

Tom Lee's heroism was matched by the courage and selflessness of those whom he rescued. For example, A. M. Lund of Little Rock, almost unconscious from his own ordeal, dived out of the *Zev* while he was being taken to shore in order to rescue someone who was floating under the water. He found the victim already dead, however, and had to struggle against the current several more minutes until the *Zev* could return for him.

In all, Tom Lee took four boatloads of survivors to shore. By the time he began his last trip, the remaining victims were more scattered and considerably downstream. He found John F. Collins and J. H. Haylow floating further down the river as they clung to timbers from the steamer. Probably the last to be saved was Walter K. Stromquist, the elderly sanitary engineer of the City of Memphis, who was holding to a life preserver. He had been in the water about an hour. Several other survivors either drifted ashore or later were picked up farther down the river.

After bringing his last group to shore, Tom Lee turned his attention to the needs of those he had saved. They were in dire circumstances. The sun had set, and they were weak from shock and exhaustion. The more feeble ones laid down and covered themselves with sand to conserve body heat. Several tried to warm a young child whose skin was blue from the cold, while others sought unsuccessfully to resuscitate a 10-year-old boy who had drowned. Running along the banks, Tom Lee collected driftwood and built a large fire to warm the victims. Soon afterward someone discovered a small house nearby, the residence of a black family, and some of the survivors made their way to it for shelter.

Their savior, however, had disappeared. He was to spend a sleepless night in the *Zev,* searching the river banks for those who had drowned. Tom Lee had a personal understanding of the terrors of drowning. *He could not swim.*

Tom Lee had completed his heroic service to those he found struggling in the water. His aid was no longer necessary, for, as news of the disaster spread, relief expeditions converged on the area. One of the survivors reached a telephone and placed a call to

Memphis. Within 15 minutes a fast motor launch, the *Elf,* sped out of the Memphis harbor with Dr. Louis LeRoy, an experienced surgeon, and two reporters for *The Commercial Appeal.* By 7:00 p.m. they had reached the group of wet and oil-soaked survivors huddled around their bonfire on the river bank. Others were gathered in the small house a short distance away, about 12 of them needing medical attention. Soon after the *Elf* left Memphis, ambulances from almost every funeral home in the city began racing southward over the Mississippi roads. They brought the first passengers back to the city. When the *Choctaw* reached Memphis about 6:15 p.m., its captain was notified of the sinking. He quickly started back down river — with medical personnel rushed by police cars from Memphis hospitals. Word of the disaster spread rapidly through the city. Large crowds were soon gathering at the waterfront and blocking streets around the Baptist and General hospitals and the offices of *The Commercial Appeal.*

Other aid began arriving from downstream. The *Monator,* a small government boat on the way upstream, was the first. Next came the *Mississippi,* a large government boat which had been moored several miles below the site. It arrived about 8:00 p.m., after its captain had seen chairs and porthole framings float by, followed by a large oil slick. Soon afterward the *Gulfport,* on its way up river, joined the search. During the night other government vessels gathered to search for bodies and aid in locating the hulk of the *Norman.*

The next morning the Corps of Engineers, with its more extensive resources, began its own search for the ill-fated boat. The Corps intended either to raise the *Norman* or to send navy divers down in a quest for more bodies. This effort was unsuccessful. Despite a thorough search with the best equipment available, the wreckage of the *Norman* was never discovered. Probably it soon was buried by the massive quantities of sand carried by the currents of the Mississippi River. However, the bodies of some of the 23 who died were recovered. They continued to be discovered along the banks downstream for several days afterward. The bones of the others remain lost, as do those of the many other victims of wrecks and drownings on the great river.

There could be no doubt of the extent of Tom Lee's heroism.

He acted quickly, calmly, and without regard to his own safety. Of the 72 people aboard the *Norman* when it began the trip toward Memphis, he had saved 32 from death. Only 17 managed to reach shore without his aid. Those he had saved had no question of their obligation to the modest hero. They embarrassed him by repeatedly shaking his hands, calling him their savior, and assuring him he would be well repaid. The Memphis press also heralded him as a hero. Probably all societies have sought to give appropriate recognition to members who have performed heroically in major disasters, and the sinking of the *Norman* also resulted in talk of an award for heroism. A Carnegie Hero's Medal was suggested but was never awarded.

But he was not forgotten. The city of Memphis, according to one survivor, "just did wonders for him." One city newspaper gave him a watch and chain, and the other gave him a trip to Washington to meet President Calvin Coolidge. Learning of his desire to own a small cabin, the Engineer Club and *The Commercial Appeal* raised more than $3,000 and bought and repaired for him a small home at 923 North Mansfield in Memphis. Discovering, when Tom Lee and his wife prepared to move into the house, that they had no furniture, citizens of the city collected used furniture and supplied the home for him. The money left after the purchase of the house was placed in a trust fund to assure the payment of insurance and taxes on it. The hero and his wife finally had a place where they could live, plant a garden, and raise chickens.

It was in this home that Tom Lee lived for the remaining 27 years of his life. For several years he worked as a laborer, earning 20 cents an hour when he could find work. Later a member of the Engineers Club secured a steady job for him—collecting garbage for the city of Memphis. His wife took in ironing. When he was allowed to retire early in 1948, already ill with cancer, he was earning $115 per month. Friends in the city government arranged a "generous" retirement of $75 monthly, a sum larger than that for which he would ordinarly have been eligible. The city previously had named a swimming pool for blacks for him.

His final years, as he struggled against cancer, were spent in his small house. The Engineers Club, which had collected money and Christmas gifts for him each year, arranged for free medical care,

The *M. E. Norman. Courtesy the MEMPHIS PRESS-SCIMITAR.*

but all treatments were futile. His condition worsened. Still thoughtful of others, he contributed money from his own meager store to the Cancer Fund. There was talk among officials in Memphis of finally getting a Carnegie Hero's Medal for him, but nothing was done. Early on the morning of April 1, 1952, as the willows were becoming green along the banks of the great river, the hero who had saved so many from death in cold, dark waters, died quietly in his small home in north Memphis. His widow, Margaret, later moved to California, where she apparently died in 1970, for a check sent to her there was returned unclaimed. The small house on Mansfield Street still stands, now occupied by others.

A hero's recognition, after his death, was given to him. E. H. Crump, unofficial political leader of Memphis and Shelby County, directed arrangements for a monument. Astor Park, on the bank of the Mississippi River, was enlarged and renamed Tom Lee Park. A marble spire, erected in the center of the grassy park, stands overlooking the great river. The base of the monument, in addition to the names of Crump and his committee members, bears the following inscription:

TOM LEE MEMORIAL
A VERY WORTHY NEGRO
TOM LEE WITH HIS BOAT "ZEV"
SAVED THIRTY-TWO LIVES WHEN THE
STEAMER U.S. NORMAN SANK ABOUT
TWENTY MILES BELOW MEMPHIS MAY 8,
1925—BUT HE HAS A FINER MONUMENT
THAN THIS—AN INVISIBLE ONE—A
MONUMENT OF KINDLINESS, GENEROSITY,
COURAGE AND BIGNESS OF HEART. HIS
GOOD DEEDS WERE SCATTERED EVERYWHERE
THAT DAY AND INTO ETERNITY.
THIS MONUMENT ERECTED BY THE
GRATEFUL PEOPLE OF MEMPHIS.

SUGGESTED READINGS

Material about Tom Lee is limited. Brief surveys about him appear in two books: Coppock, Paul R. *Memphis Sketches* (Memphis: Friends of Memphis and Shelby County Libraries, 1976), and Crawford, Charles W. *Yesterday's Memphis* (Miami: E. A. Seemann, 1976). Most of the information available about Lee can be found in two newspapers, the *Memphis Press-Scimitar* and *The Commercial Appeal,* and in interviews with survivors of the sinking of the *M. E. Norman.* Several interviews were published in *Memphis Construction Times,* Jan.-Feb., 1973. Others, collected by the Oral History Research Office of Memphis State University, are indexed in the Mississippi Valley Collection of the John Willard Brister Library at that institution. The only survivor of the disaster still known to be living in 1979 is James Wood, who now resides in Memphis. He provided valuable comments about the accuracy of this manuscript.

INDEX